GIRL, GET THAT CHILD SUPPORT

THE BABY MAMA'S GUIDE TO TRACKING DOWN A DEADBEAT, FINDING HIS CASH AND MAKING HIM PAY EVERY DOLLAR HE OWES YOU!

BY

CATHY MIDDLETON

PRINTED IN CANADA

Cover design by Keith Saunders—www.mariondesigns.com
Interior Design by Nancey Flowers—www.flowersinbloompublishing.com
Edited by Chandra Sparks Taylor—www.chandrasparkstaylor.com

This book is designed to provide accurate and authoritative information on the subject of child support. While all the stories and references described in the book are based on true experiences, some of the names may have been changed, some stories are compilations, and some situations have been changed slightly for educational purposes and to protect each individual's privacy. It is sold with the understanding that neither the author nor the publisher is engaged in rendering legal, accounting, or other professional services by publishing this book. As each individual situation is unique, questions relevant to child support and specific to the individual should be addressed to an appropriate professional to ensure that the situation has been evaluated carefully and appropriately. The author and publisher specifically disclaim any liability, loss, or risk that is incurred as a consequence, directly or indirectly, of the use and application of any of the contents of this work.

LCCN No: 2006 907 332
Library of Congress Cataloging-in-Publication Data
        Middleton, Cathy
Girl, Get That Child Support/ Cathy Middleton - 1st ed.
Library of Congress Control Number:

ISBN: 0-9787902-0-0

10 9 8 7 6 5 4 3 2 1
First Paperback Edition

ACKNOWLEDGMENTS

I would like to first thank God, who gave me a passion for child support law and laid it on my heart to write this book. I also thank my husband, Gregory, who supported me in my transformation from a child support attorney to a published author–I love you. To my little daughter, Shelby, whose faith in me helped push me to believe in my dream. To my mother, Virgie, who taught each of her children to reach for the stars. To my father, James, who told me to make sure I get our family name on the map. I hope this book will help me to do that, Daddy. To my lovely sisters Dietra, Michelle (deceased), and Lisa, thank you guys for not laughing at all of my crazy ideas. To my niece Jamila and nephew Jamal, God bless you both.

I also give thanks to my editor Chandra Sparks Taylor, who corrected me without end while still keeping my voice alive. Get ready, girl! I have a lot more manuscripts for you to edit. To my interior designer, Nancey Flowers. Nancey, you are brilliant. I look forward to working with you in the future. And to radio diva Wendy Williams of 107.5 WBLS, who let me share the microphone on her popular show—when other stations said no, you said yes.

To author Teri Woods who always responded to my phone calls and took time to answer my endless questions about the publishing process.

GIRL, GET THAT CHILD SUPPORT:

THE BABY MAMA'S GUIDE TO TRACKING DOWN A DEADBEAT, FINDING HIS CASH AND MAKING HIM PAY EVERY DOLLAR HE OWES YOU!

BY

CATHY MIDDLETON

CONTENTS

PREFACE   9

INTRODUCTION   13

CHAPTER 1   15
Who's Your Daddy?

CHAPTER 2   27
Getting What Belongs to You

CHAPTER 3   51
Having Your Day in Court

CHAPTER 4   67
Tracking Down Your Deadbeat Dad

CHAPTER 5   77
Making a Deadbeat Dad Do Right

CHAPTER 6   89
The Long-Distance Deadbeat

CHAPTER 7   97
Trusting Him to Do the Right Thing

CHAPTER 8   115
Child Support Abuse

CHAPTER 9   123
Games Deadbeats Play

CHAPTER 10   133
When the Payments Stop

WRAP-UP   139

GLOSSARY   141

APPENDIX   149

INDEX   181

FOOTNOTES   189

PREFACE

Ladies, when it comes to supporting their kids, some men are downright clueless. They just can't understand the bank-breaking costs involved in raising children. The guy could be rich and famous, like former New Edition band member Bobby Brown, whose ex-girlfriend Kim Ward reportedly lost her home in 2004 when he stopped paying her $5,000 a month in child support for their two children, LaPrincia and Bobby, Jr., or poor and nameless, like the man next door who's got a regular nine-to-five job. It makes no difference who he is. Some daddies are definitely deadbeats.

I am not trying to call all men dogs. In fact in the ten years I have been practicing family law, I have had the honor of representing dozens of good men. They are proud fathers who put their kids first and will freely endure any sacrifice if it will somehow benefit their little ones. Still, the sad reality is that for every "do right daddy" out there, you can find at least one other guy who would rather die than support his own offspring.

You may have seen these half-stepping men before–you can't miss them. They are usually the ones profiling around the neighborhood in pricey cars they can't afford, with gold-digging women they can't maintain. From their attitude, you would think they are made of cash, but let their baby mama ask for a few dollars for some Pampers or milk, and all of a sudden Mr. Money has a cash-flow crisis and is full of excuses: "Um, um, um, I didn't get paid this week. Catch up with me next Friday" or "Didn't I give you ten dollars last month for milk? What did you do with all that money?"

You see, sisters, some men struggle with what I like to call superficial vision. Simply put, they have an inability to see beyond the surface of any situation that involves their children. In its usual form, superficial vision manifests itself in this way: If everything appears all right with the kids, everything must be all right with them, end of discussion. If the kids look well dressed and properly fed, it's because Mama's hiding a fat pot of gold somewhere to help her hold things together, and she doesn't need any help from anyone, least of all her baby daddy. A woman could be down to her last dime and pleading with that man for a few bucks, but he won't hear a word she says or lift a finger in response. To him, if the kids have a roof over their heads, it's because their mother has a tall stack of hundred-dollar bills to prop it up with. He will completely ignore the shut-off warning from the electric company or the big fat eviction notice that has been tacked on her front door. None of this ever fazes Daddy Do Wrong. The only thing that matters to him is sliding by with another day of not having to contribute to the support of his children.

We women, however, can't afford to have superficial vision. Twenty-four hours a day, seven days a week, we are bombarded by big fat reminders of reality: the bills that never stop piling up and creditors who constantly nag us for money all force us to face the hard, cold facts about the astronomical cost of raising kids in our high-priced world. It is this painful reality, made all but unbearable by some self-centered men, that has stressed many a single mother right into an early grave.

Over the past decade, I have waged vicious child support battles on behalf of many emotionally worn-out women who have struggled alone to make a way for their children because Daddy suddenly decided he needed all of his money for himself–or better yet his new family. I have witnessed the spirits of women crumble under the humiliation of being forced to appeal to an often cold and uncaring court system to make their men take responsibility for their own flesh and blood because the men refused to do so on their own. My years of labor with these mothers has birthed each of them into the priceless and empowering knowledge that crying can depress a woman and getting violent may land her in jail, but gaining a keen understanding of the child support system and the rights of a baby mama will get her that much-needed child support check every time.

The legal knowledge I have used over the years to collect thousands of dollars for my clients has been stuffed into this book. I am confident that after reading it, you will be armed with the tools you need to get that child support.

ꟼNTRODUCTION

Whether you know it or not, parenting is a joint undertaking. Providing for the financial needs of children belongs to both parties–not just one–and just as a baby cannot be more her mother's child than she is her father's, the obligation to feed and clothe a kid is no greater the duty of one person over the other; both individuals are equally responsible. Yet despite this obvious fact, each day countless parents–mostly mothers–end up getting "stiffed" when it comes to supporting their kids. Their situation can be likened to a person who gets wined and dined at a five-star restaurant only to have her companion slip out the back door just as the waiter arrives with the bill, only this bill likes to eat, grows bigger every day and sticks around for at least eighteen years.

A lot of single parents who find themselves in this unfortunate situation believe that the only thing they can do is throw up their hands, shake their heads and resign themselves to a life burdened by needless financial pressure, but others, refusing to be taken advantage of stand up for themselves and their children and say no way. *Girl, Get That Child Support: The Baby Mama's Guide to Tracking Down a Deadbeat, Finding His Cash and Making Him Pay Every*

Dollar He Owes You was written just for these people, and although this book primarily addresses women, it is a useful tool for any person–mother or father–who is either seeking child support for the first time or who is already getting a support award but needs more money.

Girl, Get That Child Support offers step-by-step legal advice on each phase of the child support process from proving paternity to tracking down the money and how to use both the court and state agencies to accomplish that goal. The book is a roadmap through the complex and often confusing maze that is our nation's child support system.

Each chapter opens with penetrating questions presented to me by real-life clients during consultations that I have conducted over my ten years of practice in family law. Some of the inquiries are commonly asked by people facing child support issues, so their popularity made it crucial that they be included in this book. Others were asked only a few times in the course of my practice, yet they were so provocative, I felt compelled to include them. I follow each question with a brief answer but each chapter goes into more detail. Through these questions and the expansive answers laid out in the chapters, I hope to pull back the shroud of mystery that has long covered the child support process and make it more user friendly to everyone who encounters it. It is my sincere hope that *Girl, Get That Child Support* will empower you to stand up to the deadbeat in your life and will help you make him financially accountable to your children.

CHAPTER 1

WHO'S YOUR DADDY?

Attorney Middleton,

My world is falling apart. Last month my man left me and my son, Jason, for some woman who lives down the hall. He stopped helping me with the rent and won't even pay his half of Jason's daycare center fees anymore. Now I'm stuck paying all these bills on my little $600 a week paycheck. Over and over, I have begged this idiot to help me, but he keeps saying no, and to top it all off, yesterday he told me that he no longer thinks Jason is his child and wants him to take a paternity test. I have been with this man for the past five years. Can he really do this to me now?

Trena Benjamin

I understand how difficult your situation is, but under the law, unless this man is your husband or your son's daddy, he can walk out on you, your baby and your bills any time he pleases.

FAMILY MATTERS

Today's families are nothing like the ones who lived back in the day. Old-school households consisted of a husband and wife and their children, which they brought into the world together. New-millennium families are a lot more creative. Some couples marry, have children and spend a lifetime together while others hook up for a while, make a few babies, split and move on to the next relationship. This change in the family structure is important because the question of your man's financial responsibility to your kids rests squarely upon who he is in relationship to them.

IS HE THEIR DADDY OR IS HE NOT?

In order to hold the man in your life responsible for the support of your children, you must first prove that he is their biological father. Over the years, I have given advice to a lot of misinformed sisters out there who wrongly believe that just because they have been living with some sugar daddy who is stuffing their pockets with a little side money from time to time, he's got to keep that money rolling her way whether he wants to or not. The sad reality is that nothing could be further from the truth. The rule of thumb on a daddy's duty to pay support is simply this: If he did not help you to conceive your child, he does not have to help you to feed your child. A guy could have been handing you his entire paycheck from the time your children were born. Your kids may call him Daddy and even make school projects for him on Father's Day, but unless you can prove with a 99.5% degree of scientific certainty that he is their paternal parent, forget about getting any child support out of him.

MAKING THE CONNECTION

Paternity is the biological relationship between a father and his child.

Establishing paternity is the process of making that kinship legal. To legalize this connection, the first thing you will need to do is get a summons and petition for paternity and file them with your local family court. The summons and petition are documents that, in effect, demand a man to appear in court to answer your allegation that on a particular date, at a particular time, he impregnated you, causing you to give birth to his child. You can get summons and petition forms at your local family court or by downloading them from your court's website. Forms are also available at your state's office for child support enforcement. The address and telephone number for each state's child support enforcement agency are located in the appendix of this book.

Once your summons and petition have been filed, a copy of them must be served upon your baby daddy. A word to all you do-it-yourself sisters out there: There are lots of things in this world that you can do on your own, but serving your court papers is not one of them. You need to get your papers served by someone besides yourself who is at least eighteen years old who is not a party to your case. That means that your nineteen-year-old child for whom you are trying to get child support cannot serve her daddy. Any other adult members of your family, however, are suitable for the job. Just make sure that your relative follows the proper procedure for service of process. In most states, that means your papers must be personally served upon your man or another adult at his home or place of employment, with a second copy being sent to him by certified mail. Your relative must also fill out and sign a document known as an affidavit of service. This is simply written proof that your baby daddy received your court papers. That way, if he decides to blow off his court appearance, the support magistrate will be aware that his absence was intentional. Be sure to have your relative fill out the affidavit correctly. Failure to do so could result in your case being thrown out of court. Affidavit forms can be found at your local family court or office for child support enforcement.

Your other alternative for service is to hire a professional process server. The benefit of using a professional is that he is an expert in the methods for effectuating proper service and completing affidavits of service so you are not likely to face problems in court over the issue of how your child's father received your papers. The downside to this method, however, is the cost. Process-server fees can range from forty to four hundred dollars, depending upon how far away your baby daddy lives and how difficult it is to serve him. Be sure you are ready to put out a few dollar bills before you choose this method.

Your final alternative for serving your papers is to let your local city marshal do the job for you. A marshal is a law enforcement officer, much like a sheriff or constable. You can make arrangements to secure a marshal's services through the office for child support enforcement. Simply let the clerk there know that this is what you want, and he will take care of the rest. The upside to using the marshal is that it is free. The downside is that the marshal will only serve your papers during regular business hours, so if you fail to provide him with an address where your baby daddy can be reached between the hours of 9:00 A.M. and 5:00 P.M., you will be out of luck.

MARRIAGE AND PATERNITY TESTS

If your man was married to you at the time that your baby was conceived, congratulations. You can bypass the paternity suit. The law in most states presumes that any child you had during your marriage is also the child of your husband. The two of you may not have hit the sheets in years, you may both be with new lovers and have no intention of getting back together, yet if the two of you have not divorced, he is presumed to be the father of your child. The law in most states, however, does give your husband the right to request a paternity test if he has a concrete reason to believe that the child does not belong to him. Some courts, however, will not entertain a man's request for testing where the child in question is pushing eighteen. Paternity testing for children over the age of eighteen is against public policy because the emotional trauma associated with it can leave them scared for life.

THE COURT PROCESS

Some time after your papers have been served upon your baby daddy, the two of you will be asked to appear in court before a child support magistrate. A magistrate is not really a judge, but a lawyer who has been issued quasi-judicial powers by the state to preside over child support cases, issue orders and render decisions on matters that come before her. The first order the magistrate will make is to require you, your baby daddy and your baby to take a paternity test. She will select the facility where the test will be conducted and will issue a date and time when you are to report for testing. When you go for your test, be sure to bring along your photo I.D. and copies of your child's birth certificate. Labs are always concerned about people falsifying paternity tests, so unless you bring proof of who you are, you will not be permitted to be tested.

Approximately six weeks after all of you have taken the genetic test, the support magistrate will order you to return to court. At that time, the results of your test will be officially revealed to you. If the results show that the man really is your baby daddy, the magistrate will issue to you an order of filiation, which declares to the world that your baby daddy has been found to be the biological father of your child. The order of filiation is your official passport to the land of child support payments.

HOW THE PATERNITY TEST IS CONDUCTED

To determine if a man is your baby daddy, most labs utilize a blood genetic marker or DNA test. This test compares the DNA material of your baby and your suspected baby daddy to see whether there is a match between them. The greater the similarity in the father and child's genetic material, the greater the likelihood that he is the baby's biological father. The lesser the similarities between their material, the smaller the likelihood, and he will be excluded as the probable father of your child. The lab also tests your genetic material to insure that it secures a complete picture of your child's genetic makeup.

To secure genetic or DNA material, laboratories conduct a buccal swab test. This is painless and involves the rubbing of a long Q-tip along the inside of the mouth for the purpose of collecting your cells, which are then removed from the Q-tip and put through a scientific process. They are compared to cells or DNA material from other people to determine whether a match exists between your child and the man who you believe to be your baby daddy.

PATERNITY TEST FEES

Taking a paternity test may be simple, but paying for it can be a bit complicated. Labs generally charge anywhere from $300 to $400 for each individual who is examined, so expect the bill to swell to around $1,200 once all three of you have been tested. Traditionally, testing costs are supposed to be paid by the person who files the paternity petition, which of course, will be you. If you are well-to-do like Jennifer Lopez or Oprah Winfrey, then you have nothing to worry about. For those of more modest means , you will need to have a large mouth to make up for your tiny pocketbook. Speak up right after you are sworn in by the court officer if you cannot afford to pay the testing fees. Let the support magistrate know that you are financially strapped and could use some help. She can order your baby daddy to split the bill with you or direct a qualified public health officer to conduct the examination for free. The magistrate can also order that payment for the tests be made from public funds instead of your personal ones. If your state orders your paternity test–for example, you have a welfare case–it will automatically pay for the testing.

DO-IT-YOURSELF PATERNITY TESTING

In recent years, a host of discount testing laboratories have appeared across the nation that promise to do paternity testing at rock-bottom prices. Many companies have even appeared on the Internet flaunting endorsements from official-sounding agencies like the American Association of Blood Banks and others, but beware, ladies, some of these companies are not legitimate. A few have actually mixed up client files, resulting in faulty test results, while others have failed to secure licensing with their local department of health. To insure that your test is both safe and accurate, have your procedure performed by a court-recognized facility.

OTHER WAYS TO ESTABLISH PATERNITY

Paternity testing is a must when a guy is being a total jerk and, despite all the evidence, just can't get it through his thick skull that he is your baby daddy. If, however, you are lucky enough to have a man who is a bit more reasonable, there are far quicker ways to settle the question of paternity.

VOLUNTARY ACKNOWLEDGMENT OF PATERNITY

One way to swiftly establish that a man is your baby daddy is by simply asking him to sign an affidavit, which is known as a voluntary acknowledgment of paternity. Federal law requires all hospital maternity wards to carry paternity acknowledgment forms, so you can have it signed right after your baby is born. Keep in mind, however, that most states have a limited time period after the baby's birth within which the affidavit of paternity can be signed. In Indiana, for example, the department of health requires that the affidavit be signed within seventy-two hours after your baby's birth. If you go beyond that time, you will be forced to get an order from a court to prove that he is the father.

Once the affidavit is signed, your baby daddy's name will automatically be placed on your baby's birth certificate. A voluntary acknowledgment of paternity becomes final after sixty days, so if after signing the forms, your baby daddy suddenly has a change of heart and decides he no longer believes the baby belongs to him, he must inform your state's department of health before this time period expires, otherwise he will be forced go to court to be heard on this matter.

VOLUNTARY DECLARATION OF PATERNITY

Even if it is too late to get your baby daddy to sign an affidavit, you can still establish paternity without undergoing testing. The two of you can appear in court and swear under oath that you had sexual intercourse, you conceived and a child was born. The court will then enter an order of filiation stating that the man is your baby daddy.

BIRTH CERTIFICATES

No matter what you may have heard, ladies, simply placing your man's name on your baby's birth certificate in the absence of him signing an affidavit or a court issuing you an order of filiation, is not a legally recognized method of establishing paternity. So many women have made the mistake of believing this is enough only to discover when they seek child support that their case has been blocked for failure to legally establish a particular man is their baby's daddy.

THE BENEFITS OF ESTABLISHING PATERNITY

Establishing paternity has many benefits. Not only does it settle the question of who your baby's daddy really is, but it also entitles your child to a host of financial benefits in addition to basic child support. They include:

1.) Social Security payments to your child should her daddy die.
2.) An inheritance in his estate even if he dies without a will.
3.) Daddy's military benefits if he served in the armed forces.
4.) Insurance coverage under his health plan.
5.) Dependent benefits under state worker's compensation laws if her daddy gets injured on his job.

Each of these items can go a long way toward enhancing your child's financial status and will allow her to enjoy a secure and comfortable childhood.

CHAPTER 2

GETTING WHAT BELONGS TO YOU

Attorney Middleton,

   Ever since my daughter was five years old, her father has been giving me a bag of groceries and box of Chinese food. Every Friday evening, come rain or shine, that man will be at my front door with those groceries and that shrimp fried rice for Shawna. Now I appreciate what he is trying to do and all, but my daughter needs way more than some food. Shawna is thirteen years old now. She stands five feet eight inches tall, wears a woman's size twelve and just graduated to a size D bra cup. She can eat a bag of groceries in three days, depending upon what is in there. I also have to pay sixty dollars a week to her math tutor and twenty dollars a week for her piano lessons, and don't even ask me about the money I lay out for the girl's clothes. It's crazy. I have tried to talk to her father about it, but all he does is throw a few extra items in the grocery bag. This is bad, but as messed up as things are, I'm afraid to take him to court for more help. All my girlfriends keep calling me a gold digger. They say that a judge could even end up giving me less than I'm getting right now, and Lord knows I can barely make it with that. What should I do?

Angela Hamilton

Don't waste any more time with this man. He has absolutely no intention of giving you any meaningful help. You need to take that guy to court and get some real child support.

WHAT IS CHILD SUPPORT?

Child support is money your baby daddy has to put into your pocket to help you cover the costs of raising your child. You get only one regular periodic payment but that money is broken into two separate parts. The first is a preset percentage of your baby daddy's income, which is his share for things like food, clothing, shelter, heat, etc. The second part is money he owes you for additional or add-on expenses not encompassed in the basic child support award, like daycare center fees, tutor fees, babysitting expenses, school bus bills and summer camp.

Unless you and your baby daddy agree otherwise, both parts of the child support payment must be made in the form of money. Bottles of Similac, boxes of Pampers and bags of groceries may sound really nice, but they don't qualify as child support under the law, so please, ladies, don't let some cheapskate man convince you that he is helping you out just because he comes by now and then with a bag full of this stuff. Bringing over little knickknacks may make him feel responsible, but it doesn't even begin to cover your child's real needs.

A study conducted by The United States Department of Agriculture revealed that the average cost of raising an infant, born in 1999, from birth to eighteen years will be staggering $245,000, and if that child has any special medical or psychological needs, the cost will be even greater. A consistent flow of money from your baby daddy is the only way to put a dent in a bill this big, plus the money will do a lot more for your peace of mind than a bag of groceries. Below is a list of the usual child-related expenses courts consider when determining a support award. To ensure that you include all of the expenses in your home, fill out the monthly expense sheet on the next page.

CHILD-RELATED EXPENDITURES COURTS CONSIDER WHEN CALCULATING A CHILD SUPPORT AWARD

1.) Daycare/baby-sitter fees
2.) Transportation expenses
3.) Dry cleaning/laundry
4.) Private school tuition
5.) Health insurance
6.) Medical/dental bills
7.) Eyeglasses
8.) Food
9.) Clothes
10.) Telephone
11.) Utilities
12.) Taxes
13.) School supplies
14.) Music lessons, dance lessons and other extracurricular activities
15.) Trips and vacations
16.) Tutor fees
17.) Beauty/barber shop

MONTHLY HOUSEHOLD EXPENSE SHEET

1. Mortgage or rent $_____
   (on home or apartment)
2. Taxes $_____
   (if not included in mortgage payment)
3. Utilities $_____

4. Telephone bill $_____

5. Cable $_____

6. Food $_____

7. Garbage collection $_____

8. Car note $_____

9. Public transportation $_____

10. Clothes $_____

11. Laundry and dry cleaning $_____

12. Tuition $_____

13. Babysitting $_____

14. Daycare center $_____

15. Tutor $_____

16. Summer camp $_____

17. Medical/dental $_____
(expenses not covered by insurance)

18. Barber/beauty shop $_____

19. Extracurricular activities $_____

Total Expenditures $_____[1]

OTHER FACTORS CONSIDERED IN DETERMINING CHILD SUPPORT

Your child-related expenses are just one variable the courts will look at when determining the amount of child support you need. Other things the courts consider include: the monthly income of both parents, the standard of living your child would have enjoyed if her parents lived under one roof, the needs of any other children for which your baby daddy may be responsible and your state child support guidelines.

MOMMY AND DADDY'S INCOME

How much your baby daddy earns is a key factor that is taken into consideration when determining an appropriate child support award. Generally speaking, the bigger his paycheck, the more money you can get out of him. In some states, however, your earnings must also be considered. These states calculate child support awards by combining both parents' incomes into one figure, taking a percentage of that figure then dividing the percentage between the two parents. In Indiana, both methods are used. If your income is under $20,000, it will not be considered in calculating a child support award; however, if it exceeds this amount, your income will be combined with your baby daddy's to determine child support. We will discuss in greater detail the various approaches to calculating child support later in this chapter.

THE CHILD'S STANDARD OF LIVING

The lifestyle your child enjoyed before you broke up with her father, whether the two of you were married or not, is another major factor in determining a child support award. Support magistrates like to keep children living at the same level of luxury that they enjoyed before their parents split. It is for this reason that in 2005 rap mogul, Sean "P. Diddy" Combs, got slapped with what was arguably the biggest child support bill in the history of New York for his son Justin. Justin's mother, Misa Hilton-Brim, had earned enough money as a stylist to the stars to more than adequately provide for the boy, but it was Combs' long dollar bills that had been paying for Justin's private nanny, tuition at a top private school and trips to St. Tropez, so the court ordered Combs to keep the money flowing even though he and Hilton-Brim had long put a stop to their relationship.

YOUR BABY DADDY'S OTHER KIDS

If your baby daddy has other babies out there, then guess what, ladies? He has to support them too. After all, a man has a responsibility to all of the children he brings into this world, not just the ones that come through you, so if you are dealing with one of those real baby-making brothers, expect your checks to be a little skimpy to accommodate the needs of all those other mouths he must feed. Your best chance for getting a nice chunk out of his wallet is to push for an order of child support before his other baby mamas do. In most states, the mother who makes the first request to the court gets the most money. This is because when the court goes to calculate a father's contribution to the child it will deduct from his income other child support awards that have been previously issued against him. If the court has no knowledge of any other awards, none will be deducted, leaving you with a larger pot of money from which to take your support. Any baby mama who seeks child support after you will be forced to get her payments from whatever is left after your money comes out. There are some instances in which a man may receive a small deduction for his children who have no child support order, but to get this, he must first prove to the court that his other baby mama is making almost no money at all. Generally speaking if he hasn't been ordered to support them they don't count in court, so make it your business to file your support petition as early as possible. After all the early bird catches the fattest worms.

YOUR STATE GUIDELINES

Federal law requires each state to establish rules for determining the basic amount of support a child needs. These guidelines are simply mathematical formulas that assist courts in calculating support awards. Each state is entitled to select its own formula, however, most have adopted one of the two child support models listed below. For additional information on the guidelines your state uses, see the appendix in the back of this book.

INCOME SHARES FORMULA

The income shares formula adds your income with your baby daddy's then sets aside a percentage of that figure for child support purposes. The income shares formula rests on the assumption that both parents are equally responsible for their child and should share in the cost of supporting her. It recognizes that the parent who lives with the child uses her earnings each day to care directly for the little one while the other parent does not. So only the parent who lives outside of the home is required to pay the child support. The income shares formula is utilized in thirty-three states, including the Virgin Islands and Gaum. Income shares model states include:

Alabama	Louisiana	Oklahoma
Arizona	Maine	Oregon
California	Maryland	Pennsylvania
Colorado	Michigan	Rhode Island
Connecticut	Missouri	South Carolina
Florida	Nebraska	South Dakota
Idaho	New Hampshire	Utah
Indiana	New Jersey	Vermont
Iowa	New York	Virginia
Kansas	North Carolina	Washington
Kentucky	Ohio	West Virginia

DETERMINING CHILD SUPPORT THROUGH THE INCOME SHARES FORMULAS IS A FIVE-STEP PROCESS

Step 1: Add together the gross income of both parents.

Step 2: Look at your state guidelines to find the percentage of income that is allotted for support based upon the number of children you have.

Step 3: Add the following items to your and your baby daddy's gross incomes if they have not already been included:

* Annuity payments
* Worker's compensation
* Unemployment benefits
* Pension and retirement benefits
* Disability benefits
* Veteran's benefits

Step 4: Subtract these statutory deductions from your gross:

*Unreimbursed employee business expenses
*Alimony or maintenance payments
*Child support paid on behalf of other children
*Public assistance payments
*City income or earnings taxes actually paid
*Federal Insurance Contributions Act (FICA)
  taxes actually paid

Step 5: Calculate the prorated share that each parent owes for the support of their child. The prorated share your baby daddy owes is your child support award. The share you owe you keep since the child lives with you.

EXAMPLE 1

Let's say you and your baby daddy live in the State of New York. You each earn $50,000 a year or $4,166 a month. The two of you have one son together who is now four years old. Your child support award would be as follows:

Combined Gross Monthly Parental Income	**$8,332**
Baby mama's monthly income	$4,166
Plus baby daddy's monthly income	$4,166
Number of Children	1
Guidelines percentage of the combined gross income for one child	**17%**

The guidelines call for a basic child support obligation of $1,416 based upon 17% of the combined monthly gross income of both parents. That figure would be adjusted to account for local taxes, FICA, alimony or other deductions actually payed and then prorated between you and your baby daddy based upon your respective incomes. Since you both earn the same amount of money, each of you are responsible for a prorated share of one half of the basic child support obligation (approximately $708). Of course since the child resides with you, it is assumed that you are already exhausting your money in the form of direct household expenditures. Your baby daddy's $708, minus deductions, however, would have to be paid to you in the form of a child support award.

Your baby daddy would also be responsible for one half of any additional child- related expenses like daycare center fees, babysitting, summer camp and unreimbursed medical bills.

EXAMPLE 2

If you and your baby daddy have two kids, the New York State guidelines would call for 25% of the monthly combined parental income or $2,083. Your baby daddy's prorated share of that figure would be about $1,041, minus deductions, leaving you with this amount as your basic child support award.

PERCENTAGE-OF-INCOME FORMULA

The other method for determining child support is the percentage-of-income formula. This is the easiest way to calculate support because it simply takes a percentage of your baby daddy's income and gives it to you for child support. How much you earn has very little impact upon the award. As with the income-shares approach, states vary in terms of the method they utilize to determine your child support amount. Some will take a flat percentage of your baby daddy's income based upon the number of children while others will change that percentage depending upon his level of income. The percentage-of-income method is utilized in the following states: Alaska, Arkansas, District of Columbia (Washington, D.C.), Georgia, Illinois, Minnesota, Nevada, North Dakota, Puerto Rico, Tennessee, Texas, Wisconsin and Wyoming.

DETERMINING CHILD SUPPORT UNDER THE PERCENTAGE-OF-INCOME METHOD INVOLVES A THREE-STEP PROCESS:

Step 1: Find out your baby daddy's gross income.

Step 2: Review your state child support guidelines to determine the percentage due for support based upon his income level.

Step 3: Add or deduct the amounts listed below where appropriate.

ADD

* Annuity payments
* Worker's compensation
* Unemployment benefits
* Pension and retirement benefits
* Disability benefits
* Veteran's benefits

DEDUCT

* Unreimbursed employee business expenses
* Alimony/maintenance payments
* Child support paid to other children
* Public assistance payments
* City income taxes
* Federal Insurance Contributions Act (FICA) taxes

EXAMPLE 3

Now let's say that you, your baby and your baby daddy are living in the State of Georgia. You both continue to earn the same $50,000 a year or $4,166 per month that you did when you were living in New York, but since Georgia is a percentage-of-income state, your income will not be used in the determination of a child support award. Under Georgia law, your child support award would be calculated as follows:

Your baby daddy's monthly income	$4,166
Number of children	1
Guidelines percentage of your baby daddy's income	12%–23%

Under the Georgia guidelines you would be entitled to receive at least $499 in monthly child support and as much as $958, provided that you can prove that the needs of your child and the financial demands of your household justify the higher award.

EXAMPLE 4

If you and your baby daddy have two kids, then your child support award based upon the Georgia guidelines would be at least 23% and possibly as high as 28% of your baby daddy's income, depending upon your situation. That means you could get anywhere from approximately $958 to $1,166 per month based upon the needs of your children.

EXAMPLE 5

If you and your baby daddy decided to relocate to Washington, D.C., you would continue to receive a percentage of his income but the D.C. guidelines would provide for the calculation of child support in a much different way. D.C. support guidelines are split into five income levels, and a different support percentage is applied at each level. For example:

LEVEL 1

If your baby daddy is a Level 1, he is earning a yearly income of $7,500 or less. This man will be considered unable to contribute support in accordance with the guidelines. Therefore he will only be ordered to pay an amount that he can afford. That payment will be at least $50 per month.

LEVEL 2

If your baby daddy is a Level 2, he is earning at least $7,501 per year, but no more than $15,000 annually. As long as his payment of child support will not push him below the poverty level, he will be made to pay the following percentages for basic child support:

One child	20%
Two children	26%
Three children	30%
Four or more children	32%

LEVEL 3

A Level 3 baby daddy earns at least $15,001 per year and no more than $25,000 annually. As long as his payment of child support will not push him into poverty, he will be made to pay the following percentages for basic child support:

One child	21%
Two children	27%
Three children	31%
Four or more children	33%

LEVEL 4

A Level 4 baby daddy makes more than $25,001 per year but less than $51,000 per year. He will be made to pay the following percentages for basic child support:

One child	22%
Two children	28%
Three children	32%
Four or more children	34%

LEVEL 5

A Level 5 baby daddy earns more than $50,001 per year but not more than $75,000 per year. He will be made to pay the following percentages for basic child support:

One child	23%
Two children	29%
Three children	33%
Four or more children	35%

The District of Columbia child support guidelines do not apply to a baby daddy who is earning more than $75,000 per year. Under those circumstances child support is determined on a case-by-case basis. It should be pointed out, however, that the amount of child support that might be awarded won't be less than the amount that would be awarded where your baby daddy's income is less than $75,000.

Under the fact pattern presented earlier, your baby daddy would be a Level 4, entitling you to anywhere from about $916 to $1,416, per month depending upon your situation. The District of Columbia will also increase your child support award as your child grows older. To find out more about the child support guidelines in your state, see the appendix.

DEFINING INCOME

Income, for purposes of establishing a child support award, is far more than the mere paycheck one gets after a hard day's work. It also includes:

* Worker's compensation
* Disability benefits
* Unemployment benefits
* Social Security benefits
* Veteran's benefits
* Pension and retirement benefits
* Fellowships and stipends
* Annuity payments
* Rent received by a landlord
* Dividends from stock ownership
* Interest from a bank account
* Recording artist royalties
* Bonuses
* Overtime

THE DADDY WHO REPORTS NO INCOME

Most women with a baby daddy who gets paid by his employer in cash or simply doesn't report income assume they can't get any child support. The truth is, however, you can get just as much out of the daddy who is paid off the books as you can from one whose income is reported to the Internal Revenue Service (IRS). Even if a man has never filed a tax return or works for himself and stashes all his money in his mattress, you can still get your child support. Of course, your quest for his cash will have to be a bit more creative than if he were working on a regular job and reporting his earnings, but with a little craftiness and a bit of help, you can definitely uncover his hidden pot of gold.

SHOW ME THE MONEY

In order to get a child support magistrate to award you money from a man who is crying broke, you must first convince her that he's only pretending to be penniless and is actually hiding his money from you. Start by checking out his lifestyle. Does he own a home, rent an apartment or lease a car? Does he have a side business or own commercial property? if he does, you can use these things as proof that he has a source of money somewhere that is sustaining him. A child support magistrate will then take this and any other information you can find about his lifestyle to impute income to him. Imputing income means that the magistrate will estimate his probable earnings based upon his obvious expenditures and will award support to you on that basis.

To help the court have as clear an idea as possible about your baby daddy's income and assets, try to get pictures of things like his car or motorcycle. If you can't get pictures, run a search of his name and license plate with your local Department of Motor Vehicles (DMV). It will reveal every vehicle he owns. Most state DMV's make this information available to the public free of charge. You should also do a name search with your local office of deeds. This agency will be able to tell you whether he owns any property and how much each piece is worth. Like the DMV, deed offices allow their records to be open to the public so you will have no problem finding out what he really owns. My office recently was involved in a case with a mother whose ex quit his $50,000 a year job with the city, sold his $300,000 home and moved into his mother's basement, all for the purpose of shirking his child support obligation. To his surprise when the court calculated the support award it ignored the man's claims of pennilessness. The support magistrate chose instead to focus on a deed the woman presented that revealed that despite his lack of a job or a home, the man had just purchased a three-story building in Brooklyn worth almost $600,000. Taking the time to secure her ex's deed won this mother a child support award totaling $650 a month.

If you know your baby daddy's Social Security number, date of birth and other private facts, such as his mother's maiden name, you can get his credit report. There are a host of websites available to help you obtain this document. For a free copy of his credit report, visit www.anuualcreditreport.com or www.creditreport.com. You can also get the report by visiting the websites of the three major credit bureaus, Equifax, Transunion and Experian. If you can't get his credit report on your own, go to your local child support enforcement office. Someone there will run a credit search for you free of charge.

The benefit of the credit report is that it will give you a history of his recent purchases and loans, all of which can help you to prove that even though your baby daddy is crying broke, he has plenty of money to spend on himself.

ITEMS THAT WILL HELP YOU PROVE YOUR BABY DADDY HAS HIDDEN EARNINGS

1.) HIS CAR: Even if it is old, it can serve as proof that he has some money. He has to pay insurance on it, in addition to maintenance, and the money for this must come from somewhere.

2.) HIS HOME ADDRESS: Whether he owns or rents, he has got to pay money in order to keep a roof over his head. If he owns the house, get a copy of the deed from your local office of deeds.

3.) HIS BUSINESS INFORMATION: If your baby daddy has a business, get everything you can on it to show to the court. Business cards, fliers, phone book listings, advertisements, receipts for former customers and pictures are all good ways to show that the business exists.

4.) HIS CLOTHES: If he is always wearing Timberlands, DKNY and other designer stuff, take note of that. Get some pictures of him, if possible. He may argue that they are either gifts or were purchased on sale, but the bigger his designer wardrobe, the harder it will be for the court to believe that everything he wears was purchased at a discount or given as gifts.

5.) HIS LIFESTYLE: Does your baby daddy throw a lot of money away on parties and clubs? Does he take a lot of trips? Does he belong to a pricey gym? If he does, collect whatever proof you can concerning his lifestyle. It will help you to prove that he has extra money to spend on himself and can certainly afford to support his child.

6.) HIS CREDIT HISTORY: Did he recently lease a new car, buy a flat-screen television or secure a home improvement loan? This information can serve as great proof that he has enough money for the things he wants although he tells the court that he is broke.

HIS NEW WOMAN'S INCOME

A lot of mothers wrongly assume that if their baby daddy's has remarried, the income of his new woman can also be added to the child support pot, allowing them to secure an even bigger support award. While such an notion might sound wonderful, it is simply not true. The legal obligation to support a child lies exclusively with the biological parents of that child and no one else. Stepparents have no legal duty to help in the payment of child support, so don't expect your baby daddy's new rich wife to help him keep up with his child support payments.

THE JOBLESS DADDY

Some baby daddys are just plain lazy. They act like a job is supposed to come searching for them instead of them looking for work. In the old days, the courts would tolerate chronic joblessness, but today courts have grown more impatient. Child support magistrates throughout the nation are now ordering unemployed fathers to get off their butts and search for employment. They are also requiring those who are habitually unemployed to submit written proof that they are at least job hunting. These job search diaries, as they are called, must contain the name and address of the company where employment was sought, the company representative who the daddy contacted for the job, the date he inquired about employment and the results of his inquiry. Fathers who fail to make a good-faith effort at landing a job can end up being thrown in jail. Some courts are also beginning to set up their own job search programs for chronically unemployed fathers. Any baby daddy who disobeys a judge's order to participate in one of these programs can be held in contempt of court and thrown into jail.

DADDY'S POTENTIAL INCOME

In some states, the court will also issue an order for child support based not upon what your baby daddy actually earns, but what he should be making. This will happen when he either has no job or one that is beneath his level of skill and training. A child support award based upon potential income will factor in the parent's work history, education, qualifications and the job opportunities available to him. So if your baby daddy has a college degree, he'll be forced to pay you a support award that is equal to the income of any other college-educated person, even if he only works at McDonald's. Potential income, however, will not be considered where your baby daddy is physically or mentally incapacitated or if he is caring for a child under the age of two years, for whom he is legally responsible.

BANKRUPTCY

Even if your baby daddy files for bankruptcy, he still has an obligation to pay child support. United States Code, Section 523(a) (5) states that child support is not dischargeable in bankruptcy.

TAXES AND CHILD SUPPORT

You cannot be taxed for the child support you receive and your baby daddy cannot receive a write off for the money that he pays you. You should also keep in mind that as long as you have custody of your child, you are the only one who can claim her on your taxes, so if your baby daddy is pushing for that tax break, tell him to back off.

CHAPTER 3

¶AVING YOUR DAY IN COURT

Attorney Middleton,

I have been separated from my ex-husband for four years now. I am interested in getting child support from him for our two boys, and I really don't know how to go about it. Jimmy works as a file clerk for the city. He lives in a little matchbox apartment about a block away from my house, and I know he does not own any property. The most expensive thing he has is a 2005 Ford 500. How should I go about handling this case?

Shandrika Henderson

You need to give me a bit more information about his finances than you have so far, but assuming you know exactly what he earns and precisely what he owns, your best bet may be to save a few bucks by going to your state agency or handling your case by yourself.

HOW TO HANDLE YOUR CASE

Once you decide to sue your baby daddy for child support, the next thing you need to determine is how you will go about the process of getting your money. You have three options: You can allow your state to handle your case administratively, hire an attorney to handle your case or represent yourself. The basic filing procedures are the same for all three methods. What will differ, however, is the amount of control you maintain over things, the level of work you will have to put into the case and the size of your child support award once your case is done.

STATE AGENCY METHOD

If you want your state to handle your child support case, call your local office for child support enforcement, also known as an IV-D agency. A state-by-state listing of this agency's telephone numbers and addresses is located in the appendix of this book. When you contact them, request that an application packet for child support or paternity be mailed to you. Under federal law these forms must be sent to you within five days of your request. You can also pick up a packet at your local family court. You should receive: petitions and summonses for paternity and child support, an affidavit of service, an affidavit of financial disclosure (in combined income states only) and, instructions on how to complete each of these documents. The agency will also need certain important items from you. These include:

1.) Your child's birth certificate
2.) Your child's Social Security number
3.) Your marriage license, if your baby daddy was your husband when your child was conceived

4.) An acknowledgment of paternity or order of filiation

5.) Your identification

6.) Your Social Security number

7.) Your baby daddy's Social Security number

8.) Your baby daddy's last home address

9.) Your baby daddy's last place of employment

10.) A recent photograph of your baby daddy [2]

Be sure to give the agency copies of these items only. You should always keep your originals. Trust me, you will need them later.

Once you have completed your application and pulled together all of your documents, you are ready to submit them to the agency. Someone will process your papers and assign a caseworker to your file. The caseworker is your guide as she will accompany you through every phase of the child support process. She will help you to settle paternity, get your support papers served, establish the amount of money that is owed to you and do whatever else is needed to get your baby daddy's cash coming your way. Because your caseworker handles all aspects of your case, your court appearances will be infrequent. You will, however, have to appear in court for hearings on your matter.

Filing your case through the agency clearly has some big advantages. You can save lots of time since the agency does everything, and it is inexpensive because the agency charges no fees for the work that is done on your behalf. But agency filing has problems too. The big one is that state agencies will only track down your baby daddy's income if it is being reported to the IRS. If your baby daddy is self-employed and reports no income, or he works off the books, you are out of luck. You see, ladies, the state is not in the business of hunting down unreported income, so it won't lift a finger to help you uncover those hidden funds, including offshore bank accounts. The guy could be living like a Saudi prince while you and your kids scratch dirt to survive, yet if his tax return says he has no income, the agency will take him at his word.

The agency can also drag its feet when dealing with your case. The "red tape" that slows down most bureaucratic institutions also plagues most child support enforcement offices. You could be waiting several weeks or even months before those support checks start rolling in and, even when they do, the agency at times can fail to send the correct amount. So exercise a lot of patience when choosing this method for handling your support problems.

HIRING AN ATTORNEY

Another way to get your child support is to simply hire an attorney. Like the agency, the lawyer will handle all phases of your case from beginning to end. Unlike the agency, however, a good lawyer can get your case resolved relatively quickly—in six to eight weeks in noncomplex matters. What's more, if your baby daddy is not reporting his income, you need not worry. The lawyer will hire a private investigator to uncover his stash. This is reportedly what happened to former KISS band manager, Jesse Hilsen, who was tracked down by his ex-wife after he fled from the United States to dodge a $500,000 child support bill. Hilsen allegedly changed his name nine times as he hopped from country to country trying to hide huge sums of money he received for work he had done for KISS. Luckily through careful surveillance and dogged determination, Hilsen's ex-wife's attorney hired an investigator who uncovered his whereabouts and alerted the authorities. As of the writing of this book, Hilsen reportedly sits in a federal prison in New York for breaking federal deadbeat dad laws.

There is, however, one downside to hiring an attorney: the cost. Depending upon who you retain, legal fees can be pretty pricey. Most lawyers charge a rate ranging from $75 to $300 per hour for support cases, and if they use a private investigator, expect those fees to double. To get a good lawyer at a reasonable price, you really need to shop around. The best way to do this is by getting recommendations from former clients before retaining the attorney; also, ask if the lawyer is willing to accept a payment plan or even a reduced fee.

HANDLING YOUR CASE ON YOUR OWN

Your final option is to proceed with your case on your own. Securing child support this way will free you from fat legal fees and the snail's pace movement of the state agency. You may even be able to win the same support award you would have gotten through the other two filing methods. Doing it yourself, however, can also end up being your worse nightmare.

Representing yourself is not an easy undertaking. The child support process can be both painful and time consuming. Court hours are usually from 9:00 A.M. to 5:00 P.M., so expect to take an hour or two from work just to get your papers filed. Additionally, the family courts in most large cities are extremely crowded, which means there is a good chance you will have to sit around the court all day before you are seen by a court clerk.

If you decide to handle your case, make sure that you do your homework. Study the provisions of your state's child support law that are relevant to your situation, that way you won't screw up your own case. Most courts have a law library with knowledgeable staff who are more than willing to assist the public. You should also consult with an attorney who can explain the law to you in a meaningful way. Retaining a lawyer may be expensive but speaking to one can cost as little as $50 depending on where you go. Be sure to select a lawyer who really knows family law, that way she can let you in on a few strategies to help you win your case or tell you if your case is not worth pursuing.

WHICH ALTERNATIVE IS RIGHT FOR YOU?

The best alternative for filing your child support petition depends upon a number of issues. They include: your baby daddy's money, the means by which he earns his income and the complexity of your case.

YOUR BABY DADDY'S MONEY

As I've stated, your baby daddy's income, for child support purposes, includes far more than a mere paycheck. It consists of everything from interest from his bank accounts and annuities, dividends from his stocks, bonds, profits from business partnerships, rent from real estate and other items. If your baby daddy is well off and has a lot of income outside of his salary, then your best bet may be to hire an attorney with ties to an aggressive investigator who can track down every dime.

HOW HE MAKES HIS MONEY

If your baby daddy is legally employed and you know exactly what he does and where to find him, it could be a waste of good money to hire an attorney to get child support out of him. Of course you really need to be certain that there are no complicating issues surrounding your case, like other child support orders against him or that he has extraordinary expenses. Assuming that these matters do not pop up in your case, doing things on your own could be your best option. If, however, you are a little gun shy but still would like to save a few bucks, let your local child support enforcement agency take your matter for you.

THE COMPLEXITY OF YOUR CASE

By now it's pretty clear that the more complicated your case, the more likely it is that you will need a lawyer. Cases involving unreported income; a wealthy baby daddy; children with special medical, psychological or educational needs; a baby daddy who lives out of state or who has other kids should never be handled on your own. The nuances involving these situations are too overwhelming for a layman. They require the expertise of an experienced professional, so make sure you hire a family-law attorney before you enter a courtroom with a case involving any of these issues.

COURT DAY

If the agency handles your case, it is possible that you will never need to appear in court because your case could be processed administratively, depending upon where you live, instead of going through the judicial system. If, however, you choose an attorney to represent you or you represent yourself, then you better get ready because you will get your day in court.

Court day can be a frightening experience, even for the toughest among us. Most courthouses are filled with frustrated litigants struggling to understand our often confusing legal system. Adding to their difficulty are the many overworked child support magistrates who, driven to complete their bloated calendars, whisk through their cases at breakneck speed. Preparation is the only way to survive in this kind of jungle. Let's discuss some ways you can get prepared for your day in court.

PROOF OF PATERNITY

The first thing to get ready is your proof that the man you are dragging into court truly is your baby daddy. Acknowledgments of paternity, order of filiation or marriage license are the only items the magistrate will accept as evidence that he's the father. If you don't have one of these three documents, your case can be thrown out or delayed for several months.

You should also be sure to bring to court three important pieces of financial information: your most recent tax return, your most recent pay stub and an affidavit that discloses your assets and liabilities. (These forms are available at your local courthouse or office for child support enforcement.)

You may live in a state that calculates child support by taking only a percentage of the baby daddy's income and doesn't consider your salary at all, but bring your financial documents with you anyway. Issues may arise in your case that require the magistrate to consider your earnings (for example, your baby daddy's could lie to the court that you are a millionaire and do not need his money). It will be much easier to resolve those problems if your financial documents are at your fingertips and can be easily presented for examination than if you have to request that the case be put over for another day so that you can gather the documents and bring them to court.

PROOF OF CHILD-RELATED EXPENSES

If you have any bills and receipts for expenditures made on behalf of your child, make it your business to have these items with you on your court day. As stated earlier, most magistrates are swamped with too many cases and too little time. They don't have the luxury of being able to wait for you to run back home to get your papers or to give you another date to bring your stuff in, so if you don't have your bills right there for her to examine, you can forget about them being factored into your support award. Below is a list of bills that you must bring with you on your court day:

1.) Babysitting
2.) Daycare center
3.) School tuition
4.) Unreimbursed medical bills
5.) Summer camp
6.) Unreimbursed dental bills
7.) Tutor fees
8.) Eyeglasses, if not covered by insurance
9.) Prescriptions not covered by insurance
10.) Psychological counseling not covered by insurance

PREVIOUS COURT ORDERS

If you have been awarded child support in the past, you should also bring your prior order to court with you. Although the court is supposed to keep copies of your old child support paperwork on file, documents can from time to time be misplaced.

Additionally, if your prior order was issued by another court, it will not be on file and you will have to present a copy of it to the support magistrate.

EVIDENCE OF YOUR BABY DADDY'S INCOME AND ASSETS

Any item you may possess concerning your baby daddy's income and assets should also be brought to court with you. For a list of documents needed to prove to the court that he has financial resources, see Chapter 2.

THE MAGISTRATE'S DECISION

When your court day arrives, the magistrate will collect all of your documents as well as any presented by your baby daddy. She will carefully review each item, adding and subtracting figures, where necessary. The magistrate will then run the calculations through your state guidelines to determine an appropriate child support award.

TEMPORARY CHILD SUPPORT AWARDS

In some complicated cases, it can take the court a long time to determine your baby daddy's income and how much child support he should be required to pay. When this happens, the court will enter a temporary order of support so that you can receive money from him even though the court has not resolved all the issues in your case. After those issues are resolved, a permanent order for support will be issued on your behalf.

RETROACTIVE CHILD SUPPORT

Most baby mamas believe that once they file a petition for child support they are entitled to get money dating all the way back to the time their child was born. Unfortunately, this is not true. The laws in most states entitle you to child support dating back only to the filing of your petition. Any period prior to that time is lost as far as child support is concerned, so ladies, file your petition for child support as soon after your child is born as possible.

CHILD SUPPORT ARREARS

The money that you are awarded for the time between the date that you filed your petition for support and the date when you finally get a child support award is called arrears.

Arrears can also include any other money that your baby daddy owes you, pursuant to a child support order, but fails to pay. Like any other past due bill your baby daddy cannot ignore his support arrears. If he is unable to pay all of the arrears off in a single payment, he must work out a payment plan with either the court or the office of child support enforcement. Failure to do so could land him in the local jail.

MODIFYING A CHILD SUPPORT ORDER

A support magistrate can upwardly modify (increase the award) or downwardly modify (decrease the award) where a certain amount of time has passed since you and your baby daddy's last appeared in court. Most states require the passage of at least two years before they will consider a modification of a support award, however, some states, such as Texas, require a three-year passage of time. (See appendix for the passage of time your state requires before modifying a child support award.) Of course all of the states permit modifications even sooner where there has been a substantial and unanticipated change in either you or your baby daddy's circumstances or in the circumstances of your child. Let's review some of the situations that may entitle you to be awarded an upward modification and those that might entitle your baby daddy to a downward modification.

CIRCUMSTANCES THAT ENTITLE YOU TO AN UPWARD MODIFICATION OF YOUR CHILD SUPPORT AWARD

* Your baby daddy receives a raise in his income, which would result in more than a 10% increase in your support order.

* You lose your job or experience at least a 10% decrease in your income. (In combined income states only; see Chapter 2.)

* Your child experiences a medical emergency resulting in extraordinary bills.

CIRCUMSTANCES THAT MAY ENTITLE YOUR BABY DADDY TO A DOWNWARD MODIFICATION OF YOUR CHILD SUPPORT AWARD

* Your baby daddy experiences a significant reduction in his income, through no fault of his own.

* Your baby daddy has another child.

In most states, only the court can modify a child support order. The parties cannot legally change the order on their own.

SUSPENSION OF A CHILD SUPPORT AWARD

Your child support award can also be suspended. This means that your payments can be stopped. Child support suspensions are generally granted where a baby daddy is laid off or fired through no fault of his own, or if he becomes incarcerated. As with child support modifications, a suspension cannot be legally secured without the approval of a court or your state agency.

CHAPTER 4

TRACKING DOWN YOUR DEADBEAT DAD

Attorney Middleton,

   I was awarded $800 a month in child support from my twins'
father back in 1995, but he never paid me even a fraction of that
money. The last time I saw that bum was right after our case was
over. He was outside of the courthouse, looking like a clown,
hollering at the top of his lungs that he would rather sell everything he owns and move back to Italy than give anything to a
filthy whore like me. Can you believe that? The only thing I ever
asked him to do was to take responsibility for his children, and he
calls me a whore. By now he has probably moved far away and
started a whole new family somewhere. It's like when he ended
his relationship with me, he thought that he could end his relationship with his kids too. Tell me, what can I do now?

Barbara Spinelli

   **You may think that your situation looks bleak but don't give
up yet. There are a lot of things that you can do to track down
that deadbeat and make him pay the money that he owes you.**

Trying to track down a deadbeat can be a bit like looking for a needle in a haystack. It seems that no matter how hard you search, he simply cannot be found, and in the end, frustrated by his disappearing act, you just want to give up. If you are one of the millions of women who are in the peculiar position of trying to find a "hide-and-go seek" daddy, take heart, my weary one. Your search may be almost over. There are a host of resources out there to help you, but as any good hide-and-go-seek player can tell you, you have to know where to look.

THE MORE YOU KNOW,
THE FARTHER YOU CAN GO

To insure that you get the support you deserve, you need to keep an eye on your baby daddy's important information. Some women get so preoccupied with the pursuit of trivial stuff, like the size of the guy's penis or how curly his hair is, that they will completely ignore the things that really matter. I once counseled a nineteen-year-old mother of twins who couldn't secure child support from her children's father because during their six-month relationship she never bothered to get his address, so we couldn't serve support papers on him. She could tell me everything there was to know about his hazel-colored eyes, olive-toned skin and the Latino/African heritage that accounted for what she called his "big red" appearance, but as to the address of his home or job, she was completely at a loss. Ladies, the cost of raising a child is far too high for you to be taking the kind of chances this girl did. Play it smart. Start collecting information on that man as soon as you can. Make it your business to find out the following:

SIXTEEN THINGS EVERY MAMA MUST KNOW ABOUT HER BABY DADDY

1.) His first, last and middle name–nicknames won't do
2.) His Social Security number
3.) His last known home address
4.) His last known work address
5.) His date of birth
6.) The make, model and year of his car
7.) His license plate number
8.) City and state where he was born
9.) His military record, branch of service, discharge status, dates of service, service number, service rank
10.) His last known telephone or cellular phone number
11.) His profession (Many professions require their members to register with the state and provide up-to-date information on their home and work addresses.)
12.) If he is self-employed, the names, addresses and telephone numbers of at least a few of his clients
13.) The address of any real estate that he may own
14.) If he has a criminal record, the place where he was incarcerated, dates of incarceration, his prison number, what he was convicted for, the name and address of his probation officer
15.) The full names and addresses of his parents and other relatives and friends
16.) Where he attended school and when he graduated

GETTING WHAT YOU NEED

Most men are very tight-lipped when it comes to exposing the intimate details of their lives. Few males will tell you all the juicy tidbits, especially in the early stages of your relationship. For example, a guy may tell you that he spent some time in the military, but he will skip right over his serial number or the exact dates of his service. That kind of stuff you will just have to work a little harder to get. There are a lot of men who if approached the right way will gladly open up to you. This is especially true if they are really into you. I always tell women, if he wants your sex, he ought to be willing to give you a little something too. After all, he can't expect you to trust him with your body if he's not willing to trust you with his personal information.

SEARCHING HIS BELONGINGS

Far be it for me to suggest to any woman to go snooping around in a man's things. This kind of behavior is not only deceptive but can land you in a hospital, if you get caught by a man who happens to be the violent type. That having been said, however, I don't think that there is anything wrong with taking a peek at his stuff if he either happens to have it lying around the house for anybody to see or if he has placed you in a position where you must come into close contact with his private information. For example, if he has you doing his laundry, you need to be doing a once-over of his pockets too. In fact, I strongly encourage women under these and similar circumstances to grab as much information as they can. Write down every important thing that you can find: his Social Security number, identification number at work, birthday or anything else you can get. Just be careful to hide your notes in a place where he can't uncover them later. I knew a woman who secretly found out her man's Social Security number and put it on a piece of paper that she stuffed in her handbag. Later on, when she allowed him to go through the bag in search of a piece of gum, he found the number and went ballistic.

HIS FRIENDS AND FAMILY

If your baby daddy brings you around his family members and friends, make sure you keep track of them.[3] Even if the person is only his play cousin twice removed through his in-laws on his great-grandfather's side, take note of his telephone number, address, last name and anything else of which you can get hold. You never know the role that person will play in helping you track down your baby daddy if he should decide to turn deadbeat on you. I counseled a woman from Alabama who was finally able to track down her baby daddy through a telephone call to his aunt in New York. By reaching out to his relative, she was able to secure his new address and serve him with child support papers although he had been trying to avoid her for several months.

FORMER EMPLOYERS

A former employer can also be a great source of information on a baby daddy who is missing in action. The law requires that all former employers mail a W-2 form to every employee. This means that there is a great chance that a former boss has a current mailing address for your baby daddy.

DEPARTMENT OF MOTOR VEHICLE RECORDS

Another great place to search for a baby daddy is your local Department of Motor Vehicles. The DMV in many states will provide you with information concerning his most recent address as a matter of public record. You should be aware, however, that there are a lot of states that prohibit the release of this information unless you are an attorney or law enforcement officer.[4] Of course, if your child support case is being handled by your state's child support enforcement office, you need not worry as they have direct access to all databases for all your state agencies, including the DMV.

HIS NEIGHBORS

Your MIA baby daddy won't tell you where he has disappeared and he may not report his new address to the DMV, but there is always a remote possibility that he has spilled the beans to his former neighbors, so be sure to check in on them as part of your manhunt. If you have never met them before be careful not to tell them the real reason for your search. Pretend that you want his new address for some other reason.[5] Tell them you are his long-lost sister hoping for a family reunion.[6] Say you are a friend who borrowed some cash and now you want to pay it back. You can even pretend you are from a courier service attempting to deliver a package, just try your best to be convincing.[7] If you are acquainted with the neighbors, you are going to have to be a bit more honest, after all they probably already know you are his baby mama. Expect them to take longer to open up to you, since most people like to steer clear of other folks' drama.

HIS PROFESSIONAL LICENSE

Many professions like law, medicine, nursing, and engineering require their practitioners to secure special licenses as a prerequisite for membership. The licensing agencies keep up-to-date information on their members' dates of birth, home and work addresses and other sensitive items. To find the licensing agency that may possess information on your baby daddy, call your state's department of licensing. It will provide you with the name and telephone number of the agency that may have your baby daddy's information.

HIS CRIMINAL RECORDS

A baby daddy with a criminal record should be pretty easy to track down. If you know the state and county where he was arrested, contact the department of probation there to find out the status of his case.[8] If it is still open, then you may be able to have him served with your child support papers during one of his visits with his probation officer. Even if the case is closed, the probation officer still may be willing to divulge to you his last known address or place of employment. This information will allow you to at least attempt to serve your papers, an act that will permit your case to go forward in court. The probation officer will also have your baby daddy's Social Security number and date of birth.

GOVERNMENT LOCATOR SERVICES

Both the federal government and each state have locator services that aid in tracking baby daddys who are MIA. The state locator can run database searches of the records of state agencies like the DMV, state tax department, the state board of elections, as well as his bank records and credit report. The federal locator service can conduct a search of all federal records, including military service, Social Security and the IRS. You can request both a state and federal locator search at your local child support enforcement office.

HIS CREDIT REPORT

As has already been stated in Chapter 2, credit reports can be a valuable weapon in your battle for child support.[9] They are loaded with juicy pieces of valuable, personal information that can do wonders for your case. Through a credit report you can get your baby daddy's most current address and place of employment.[10] Of course, in order to conduct the search, you must be armed with his full name—nicknames won't do—Social Security number, date of birth and even his mother's maiden name. If you have this stuff, you should be able to get his report yourself on the Internet. If for some reason you are unable to secure a report on your own, contact your state office for child support enforcement, which can conduct a free credit search on your behalf.

HIGH SCHOOL AND COLLEGE ALUMNI ASSOCIATIONS

If your baby daddy is a high school or college graduate, there's a good chance that his school's alumni association will be able to help you track him down. These organizations keep a database containing the home address, date of birth and in some instances even the place of employment of their former students. They also tend to update their information annually, so the database is kept pretty current. When contacting your baby daddy's old school, be sure not to let them know the reason for your call.[11] Instead, pretend to be his new wife, calling at his request, to find out whether they have your new address.[12] Let them read to you the address in their records first then either confirm that it is correct or give them a fake one. Have fun and be creative.

CHAPTER 5

MAKING A DEADBEAT DAD DO RIGHT

Attorney Middleton,

    I got an order for child support from the Bronx County Family Court a year ago, but I still am not receiving all of the money that I am supposed to get from Ricky. He will drop off $50 or $60 now and then and always promises to pay the rest next week, but of course he never does. The only time he ever gave me all of my money was when I got fed up and filed a petition against him for disobeying the support order. As soon as he was served with the papers, he busted into my house with every cent he owed me and then some. He started being really sweet to me too. Eventually he convinced me to drop my case against him. After that he went right back to his same old lame excuses. What should I do?

Thelma Reade

    The failure to pay child support is a very serious matter. Such conduct is illegal and can result in serious punishment. Your child's father can also be forced to pay you your child support. Stop playing with this man and haul him back to court ASAP.

Having a child support order doesn't mean squat if you're not getting paid any money, and the sad reality is, ladies, that although a whole lot of women out there have child support orders, only a fraction of them ever see the cash that has been awarded to them.[13] Studies show that less than half of all mothers who have been issued child support never collect all that money, and last year our nation's child support arrears (past due child support) soared past one billion dollars. The problem is that too many of us don't know a thing about getting our hands on those child support dollars. We allow everything from blind trust in our baby daddy to the belief that we can support our kids all by ourselves to keep us from exercising our legal rights and getting what rightfully belongs to us. If you are a sister who falls into this category then stay tuned because this chapter is definitely for you.

IT'S BUSINESS NOT PERSONAL

Child support is a financial issue, not a relationship problem. It's not about whether you want that man back or why he left or if the two of you can patch things up again. Child support is about a father meeting his financial obligations to the children he has helped to bring into this world, so be smart, sister. Don't let some slick man sweet-talk you into letting him slide without giving your kids what he owes them. Girl, make him pay by any means necessary. And if your man happens to be African-American, then whatever you do, please don't let him run any guilt trips on you about the evils of dragging a brother through a court system. Remember, if he was doing what he was supposed to do in the first place, neither one of you would need to go to court. My advice to you is to simply handle your child support case like you would any other business transaction and kick all that emotional garbage straight to the curb.

GETTING HIS MONEY

Now that we are clear that you have got to do whatever you need to do in order to make a deadbeat pay, let's turn our attention to some of the surefire methods that are guaranteed to shake that money right out of his pockets and into your purse.

THE PAYCHECK

The best place to hit a deadbeat dad is in his paycheck. This is because the money is guaranteed to come directly to you so long as he is working, and let's face it, ladies, most men must work to survive. There are basically two ways to hit a paycheck, one is by a wage withholding, the other is called a garnishment. Let's examine them both.

WAGE WITHHOLDING

A wage withholding is a court order that requires your baby daddy's job to take money from his paycheck to forward to you or your state's child support collection agency.[14] The great thing about a wage withholding is that once the job gets the copy of your child support order, they absolutely must take the money out of your baby daddy's paycheck and send it off to the proper party. Neither your baby daddy nor his boss has a choice in the matter, so you can rest assured that you are going to get your child support. The boss can't complain about the amount taken or the reason for its removal. He also cannot drag his feet when it comes to sending out the money. By law he must remove the money within ten days after receipt of the order and forward it to the proper party within thirty days.[15] Should your man get fired or up and quit his job, the old boss must let you know this, and he must pass onto your state child support collection unit any information he may have about the new employer. You can get a wage withholding through your local office of child support enforcement.

GARNISHMENT OF WAGES

A wage garnishment is an order from a court to deduct a lump-sum chunk of money from your baby daddy's paycheck to give to you. Garnishments are only issued to pay off child support arrears and involve a single payment. The benefit of a garnishment is that you get your money in one lump sum instead of having to wait to receive it in bits and pieces. [16]

TAX INTERCEPTION

You can also go after a deadbeat's tax refunds to get your child support. If your child support case was handled by your state agency or you are receiving payments through your local child support enforcement office, your baby daddy's name will automatically be submitted to your state income tax agency as well as the federal government for possible tax interception. If he is entitled to get a refund, that money will bypass his hands and get routed into the possession of your local child support enforcement agency who will ultimately forward the funds to you. To receive your baby daddy's federal tax refund, the arrears owed to you must be greater than $500, and his total refund must exceed that figure. To receive a state tax interception, arrears need only be $150.

PROPERTY GARNISHMENT

In addition to garnishing your baby daddy's paycheck and intercepting his tax refund, you can go after his other assets too. If he has a savings account, certificate of deposit or Individual Retirement Account (IRA), that money is up for grabs. In order to get your hands on it, however, you must first obtain a writ of execution. This is simply an order demanding that certain assets belonging to your baby daddy be frozen, which means that he cannot withdraw his money out of his bank account unless he gets a judge's order permitting him to do so. The more common name for the writ of execution is bank levy because it is usually used against bank accounts.[17] To freeze his assets, you must serve his bank with a writ demanding them to bar the account from any further activity and to turn over any money being held on behalf of your baby daddy to the appropriate court. You can find bank garnishment writ forms at Staples, OfficeMax and smaller office supply stores. The form must be filled out and filed with the clerk of the court. You must then serve a second copy of the writ upon the bank. Keep a final copy for yourself.

If you want to go after his personal property, you must file a writ of execution with the clerk's office and another copy with your local sheriff's office. The third copy will be served upon your baby daddy. Remember to keep a copy for your files. If your baby daddy fails to give you your money within five days (in most states) of you serving him, you can demand that the court have his property sold and the money from the sale turned over to you. But remember in order to have the property seized and sold you must provide both the sheriff and the court with a detailed description of the item you are going after. For example, if you want his car, you must give the make, model, year and vehicle identification number. You also must know where the property is located and when it will be at that location.

HOUSES AND OTHER PROPERTY

If your baby daddy owns a house or some other kind of real estate, then you can go after those things too. Remember, however, that getting money through real estate can be very a complicated task. Most states require you to secure a lien against his property, file it with the state agency that handles deed filings then get a judgment sale. You will likely need a lawyer to help you through this complicated process.[18] Still, if your man owes you a large amount of money in past-due child support, this could be the way to go. Just make sure you hire a lawyer who is an expert in both family law and real estate.

HIDDEN ASSETS

Once a man knows you are hot on his trail in search of the child support that he owes you, he is bound to try to hide his property by transferring it out of his name and into the name of somebody who is close to him like his mama or his new wife. If your baby daddy tries to pull this trick on you, fear not. There is something you can do about the situation. If you have specific information about his property, for example, you know that he once owned a house at a certain address or had an account at a particular bank, and now he's pretending to be too broke, busted and disgusted to pay you support, you can demand that the court order him to produce records dating as far back as one year concerning whatever you think he owned. He will then be required to explain to the court what happened to those items and why he does not own them now. If his explanation is in any way fishy and reveals that he has put his stuff into someone else's name to avoid paying you, then the transfer will be considered an illegal one, and you will be able to go ahead and garnish that property to get your child support.

LICENSE SUSPENSION

If your baby daddy insists upon not paying support and those arrears are starting to really pile up, your state has the power to suspend any license that has been issued to him. States differ on how much money must be owed in order to suspend licenses. For example, in New York, arrears must be as high as $5,000 before any action will be taken, while in Mississippi, failure to pay support for two months is enough to warrant a suspension. All states agree, however, that the suspension of license privileges does not only extend to driving but to a host of activities. Licenses covered by state suspension laws include: fishing, real estate, liquor, contractor, law, medicine, dentistry, social work and teaching.

JAIL TIME

Refusing to give up that money can also land your baby daddy on lock down. The failure to pay court-ordered child support is a crime under both state and federal law, and a delinquent parent will be tracked down, arrested and prosecuted like any other criminal. Additionally, under the Deadbeat Parent's Punishment Act, if your baby daddy travels across state or country lines with the intent of evading child support payments and he owes you more than $5,000 or has failed to pay for at least a year, he can be convicted of a felony and be forced to serve two years in prison.

If your deadbeat dad is a working man and he pays your child support in bits and pieces, the court can throw him into weekend jail from Friday evening to Sunday evening. This way he can keep his job and his money coming to you.

MOST WANTED LIST

Almost as humiliating as doing time in jail is finding oneself on a most wanted deadbeats list. Child support enforcement offices throughout the nation have begun to put up websites listing the worst offenders of federal and state child support laws. These men have avoided payments for several months and owe thousands of dollars in past-due support. The names that appear on the websites are placed there by the states. You can, however, request that your baby daddy's name be added to the list by contacting your local child support enforcement office. For a nationwide listing of deadbeats, visit DelinquentDad.com on the World Wide Web. This site contains state-by-state listings of men who have broken child support laws. It also contains the first and last name of each offender, the amount of support owed, his last known address and what he does for a living.

Most of the men who are posted on deadbeat sites are relatively unknown; however, celebrities have been placed on these sites as well. Recently, the State of Washington added former Seattle Seahawks running back Chris Warren to its Web page. Warren owed some $103,147 in past-due child support to the mother of his two children, ages ten and eleven.

VASECTOMY

Recently a few judges across the country have actually begun to encourage deadbeat dads to not have more children. In Newport, Kentucky, family court judge Michael "Mickey" Foellger, gave several men with multiple children and large past-due child support bills the option of either going to jail or undergoing surgical sterility. In Akron, Ohio, a Supreme Court judge warned a delinquent dad that if he did not make an effort to try not to get another woman pregnant for five years, he risked going to jail. While most judges have not adopted such drastic forms of punishment, it is becoming more popular.

CHAPTER 6

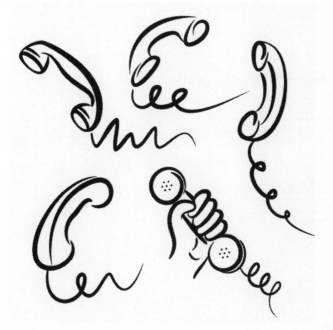

ᎢHE ᏐONG-ᎠISTᎯNCE ᎠEᎯDBEᎯT

Attorney Middleton,

My boyfriend moved to Charleston, South Carolina, six months ago and ever since he left, he has stopped paying me child support. When he was here in New York he used to always come over to my house with money and other things for the kids. He was so generous that I never felt the need to take him to court like some women are forced to do, but now that he has moved down south, I don't even hear from him, much less get any support out of him. I have tried to contact him down there but his phone is disconnected, and every time I write to him, my letters keep coming back stamped RETURNED TO SENDER, ADDRESSEE UNKNOWN. What am I supposed to do? I can't go down to South Carolina to track this man down. I simply can't afford to do that.

Aquilla Johnson

Don't pack your bags yet, girl. Believe it or not, the only trip you really need to make is the one to your local family court.

In the old days when a deadbeat skipped town, the family he left behind was simply out of luck. A mother's only hope was to track him down and file a child support petition in his new home state. Even if she was fortunate enough to already have an order for support from her own state, she would still have to plead with the courts of his state to honor that order. Most of the time her requests would fall upon deaf ears, as the other state, concerned with its statute of limitation laws, would refuse to collect child support arrears. To resolve these and other interstate child support collection issues, in 1992, the laws underwent a drastic change. Let's review these changes and discuss how they benefit you.

UNIFORM INTERSTATE FAMILY SUPPORT ACT

The Uniform Interstate Family Support Act (UIFSA) has forever changed the collection of child support across state lines. Now you can sue your baby daddy for child support, medical insurance and arrears without ever having to leave the comfort of your own state. As long as you have an order establishing paternity or support, UIFSA will allow you to go after him regardless of where he lives. Additionally, unlike the old law, your order does not have to be registered with his state child support enforcement agency. That means you can get your money more quickly than before. The act also makes it more difficult for your baby daddy's state to make changes to your support order. This means that the amount of money your state awarded you is the amount you will get from him wherever he lives.

If you failed to get an order for support against your baby daddy before he skipped town, don't worry, girl, UIFSA will allow you to sue him for paternity or support in your local court or, depending upon the type of case you have, it will allow your state to appoint a state's attorney to represent you in a proceeding conducted in his state. You will even be permitted to testify by telephone should the need arise.

The act has also eased the burden of dealing with your baby daddy's out-of-state employers. This law forces employers to honor out-of-state income deduction orders whether they want to or not. Under the law, the employer must send you the exact amount of support that you have been awarded by your local court or face an assortment of punishments, including contempt of court, fines and other penalties. [19]

GETTING STARTED UNDER UIFSA

If your baby daddy is out of state, getting support from him through UIFSA can be as easy as if he were living next door. All you have to do is take a trip to your local family court to request a UIFSA petition for paternity or child support. As with other paternity and child support cases, UIFSA cases can either be handled by your state office of child support enforcement through an attorney or you can choose to do it on your own. If the state agency handles your case, all aspects of it will be handled by them. You will have nothing to do except sit back and wait for your support. Should you, however, decide to handle your case, there are a few things you need keep in mind:

1.) To get child support in your state, your local court or child support enforcement office must first secure "long-arm jurisdiction" over your baby daddy. Long-arm jurisdiction is a legal term that simply means that the court has the right to hear a case involving your baby daddy and to order him to pay child support at the conclusion of that hearing. To secure long-arm jurisdiction, you must be able to establish that he once lived in your state or that he had sex with you in your state, causing you to become pregnant with the child for whom you are seeking support.

2.) Remember that a copy of your order or petition must be served upon him out of state. This can be satisfied under UIFSA by simply mailing a copy of your papers by certified mail, return receipt to your baby daddy, or if you have an income deduction order, by mailing a copy to his employer.

Once you have appropriately addressed these issues, your pursuit of child support under UIFSA should be a smooth experience.

DEADBEATS WHO FLEE THE COUNTRY

Some deadbeats are so outrageous they will even move overseas to avoid giving you your money. Going after child support from a baby daddy in another country can be annoying, however, under UIFSA, it is possible. Many state child support enforcement agencies have made agreements with foreign countries to recognize overseas child support judgments and to help establish child support orders where none exists. Most of the states have reciprocating agreements with Bermuda, Austria, Fiji, Jamaica, Ireland, South Africa, Canada, Nova Scotia and Mexico.

A foreign country cannot enter into a reciprocating agreement with a state unless its child support policies and procedures are similar to those used in our country. Everything from methods for establishing paternity to how child support awards are calculated and enforced must meet the same minimal standards in the United States. Moreover, just as the United States has a child support enforcement agency to carry out its guidelines, a foreign country must also designate a single agency through which its child support matters are handled.

To initiate an overseas petition for child support, you must utilize a UIFSA petition form. Your state office for child support enforcement will then file your petition with a designated child support agency in the reciprocating foreign country. That country in turn will bring a lawsuit against your baby daddy for paternity, child support or to enforce an already existing order for support. Once the case is finalized, your baby daddy's money will be collected by the overseas child support enforcement agency and forwarded to your state's office of child support enforcement, which will ultimately turn it over to you.

The federal government has also negotiated reciprocity agreements with other countries on behalf of U.S. citizens. If your baby daddy has fled to a country that has no arrangement with your state child support enforcement agency or the federal government, there still may be a chance for you to get your child support. Contact the Office of Citizens Consular Services: Department of Citizens Consular Services, Washington, D.C. 20520.

A list of countries that have reciprocating agreements with the United States is located in the appendix of this book.

CHAPTER 7

TRUSTING HIM TO DO THE RIGHT THING

Attorney Middleton,

My baby is due next month, and my boyfriend and I have been really focusing on this child support thing. He declares that he is going to be a responsible father, and he promises that he will do everything necessary to provide for his child. His one demand, however, is that I not drag him into court. You see, my man thinks that sisters are always ruining brothers' lives by dragging them through the racist justice system. He also thinks that it would be less stressful for him if we could just work things out on our own. I really don't want him to think that I am a bad person or anything, but I am afraid to believe him. I mean, a part of me wants to trust him, but the other part says that I had better forget about him and concentrate on protecting myself and my baby by taking him to court. What should I do?

Keisha Taylor

If you know what's good for you, you will forget about what he thinks and follow the little voice in your heart that tells you

to take him to court. After all, that's your common sense talking.

TO AGREE OR NOT TO AGREE

One of the most difficult challenges you will encounter as you journey through your child support experience is having to decide whether to haul your baby daddy into support court or figuring out if the two of you can enter into a settlement agreement on your own terms. Now let's not forget, ladies, a man will change his mind as often as the wind blows, so if you're not careful, he could really jerk you around on this issue. Some guys start out paying regularly only to slack off as soon as some event happens in their lives like the birth of another child, a new marriage or the purchase of a new car. Others will outright lie and say that they will pay only to end up never giving a dime. Knowing whether your baby daddy will be a responsible man or a lying cheapskate can be difficult to predict. Luckily, most men possess certain telltale character traits that, when examined closely, can definitely clue you in on whether he's got the makings of a delinquent dad or an agreement-worthy man.

IS HE WILLING TO HEAR YOU OUT?

The last time that syndicated radio personality and bestselling author Michael Baisden stepped into a Chicago family court, it was not to fight off demands for more money by his daughter's mother. On the contrary, it was to withdraw an order for support that he had faithfully obeyed for quite some time. Shortly after leaving the courthouse, Baisden's baby mama explained her decision to withdraw her demand for support during an interview on his syndicated show, *Love,*

Lust & Lies. She freely shared with listeners that Baisden, who initially had serious problems with paying child support, transformed into a financially faithful father only after she sat him down and revealed to him the many bills she had collected in order to support their daughter. Fortunately, Baisden's response to this revelation was a positive one. Rather than ignoring his daughter's mother or labeling her a gold digger, he changed his behavior and started giving her the additional money she needed. A willingness to listen as you share the financial needs of your child is a strong indicator of whether a man is agreement worthy. If your man is willing to engage in peaceful and positive discussions about his child's needs, without "going off" on you or whining about his other financial commitments, he is probably a good candidate for a child support agreement.

WHAT KIND OF DADDY IS HE?

Does your baby daddy see his child as an asset or has he branded her a liability? Does he lavish her with his time and affection, or do you find yourself always complaining about the fact that he never seems to come around?

When a guy is emotionally detached from a child, he will be financially detached from her as well. A man may empty his pockets for someone he loves, but he'll hold back every dollar he has from one who has no place in his heart, so please be honest with yourselves, ladies. If your baby daddy doesn't want to be in your child's life, you can guarantee that he's not going to have an easy time paying you child support. This bit of information may be hard to receive, but it will save you from trusting him with a child support agreement, which in the end he refuses to honor.

WAS HE THERE FOR YOU THROUGH YOUR PREGNANCY OR DID HE AVOID YOU LIKE THE PLAGUE?

How your baby daddy handles your pregnancy can be a great predictor of the kind of commitment he will have to his child once she arrives. A man who was not supportive of you, whether emotionally or financially, while you were pregnant is not likely to magically turn into the father of the year after the birth, and if he thinks that you tricked him or forced him into fatherhood, he might even be hostile toward you and your baby. My advice to you is to trash the idea of having an agreement and get yourself a child support order. The birth of your baby may be a blessed event to you, but it won't do a thing to change him from a deadbeat to a do-right.

HOW DOES HE TREAT YOU?

Some men have a real hard time showing women even the slightest amount of respect. You may be the mother of his child, yet he treats you like trash whenever you are around him. You can work like a dog caring for his children but he curses your name and calls you an unfit mother to everyone he knows. If your baby daddy treats you like a second-class citizen, recognize that he does, and don't make excuses for his behavior. A man who deals with you on this level is undeserving of your trust. Entering into an out-of-court agreement with him will only give him another opportunity to disrespect you. Avoid his drama and take him straight to court.

DRAFTING YOUR SUPPORT AGREEMENT

If after some time and reflection, you decide that your baby daddy is worthy of an out-of-court child support agreement, you must next turn your attention to putting it down on paper. A man's promise to pay may sound really convincing, but it if he should one day have a change of heart, you will be the one left broke, busted and disgusted. Be smart. Protect yourself and your child by memorializing your baby daddy's promises in a legally binding, typewritten document. That way, if he should start holding back on the money, you can hold his feet to the fire and force him to honor his word.

THE CONTENTS OF THE AGREEMENT

To create a solid child support agreement, one that effectively protects you and your child both now and later, you must address several key child support issues, including:

1.) Will your child attend private school?

2.) Will your child require daycare or babysitting services?

3.) Will you claim your child on your taxes?

4.) Does your child have special medical or psychological needs?

5.) Will your child's father be responsible for her health insurance?

6.) Will your child need to travel out of state to visit with her father? If yes, who will pay those expenses?

7.) Will your baby daddy secure a life insurance policy naming her as a beneficiary to protect her should he die before she becomes an adult?

8.) How often will payments be made and by what means will they be made?

9.) How much do you and your baby daddy earn?

YOUR STATE CHILD SUPPORT GUIDELINES

Another item that you must review to insure that your agreement is a thorough and well-written one is your state child support guidelines, which tell you exactly how much child support you are legally entitled to get from your baby daddy. Without them, you have no way of knowing whether your support agreement provides you with all the money you and your child deserve. As we discussed in Chapter 2, states differ in the methods they utilize to calculate child support awards. Some use the combined parental income method while others use the percentage of the nonresident parent's (your baby daddy's) income method. Review Chapter 2 or check the appendix to make sure you know which method your state follows. To help you determine the monthly amount, you should be receiving for child support, sample child support calculation sheets have been included in this chapter. Simply fill in each line with the appropriate information, perform the calculations where necessary, and you can determine to the exact penny your monthly child support entitlement.

HOW STATE GUIDELINES DETERMINE INCOME

In determining child support, all states calculate gross income from the following sources:
* Wages and tips
* Business profits
* Dividends
* Worker's compensation
* Unemployment benefits
* Veteran's benefits
* Fellowships and stipends

* Social Security benefits
* Pension and retirement benefits
* Alimony and maintenance
* Annuity payments

Once gross income has been calculated, you must next find out whether you live in a state that calculates child support based upon your gross income or if the calculation is made upon your net income. Gross-income states determine child support awards based strictly upon the above-listed income sources. Net-income states subtract certain deductions from the gross, creating what is known as an adjusted gross income. The following items are recognized by net-income states as deductible from gross income:

* Unreimbursed employee business expenses
* SSI (Supplemental Social Security Income)
* State or city income taxes actually made
* Child support actually paid to other children
* Alimony or maintenance payments
* FICA (Federal Insurance Contribution Act) taxes paid

COMBINED INCOME OR
PERCENTAGE-OF-INCOME STATE

Next find out whether you live in a combined parental income state or a percentage-of-income (baby daddy's income) state. If you live in one of the thirty-three states listed in Chapter 2 that combine the income of both parents in order to determine child support, then you must add your income to your baby daddy's income. If, however, you live in one of the fourteen percentage-of-income states, then move on to the next step.

APPLY THE STATUTORY PERCENTAGES

Now multiply the gross income or adjusted gross income, depending upon your state by the statutory percentages provided in your state guidelines, based upon the number of children in your household. For example, if you live in Wisconsin, your guideline percentages are as follows:

1 child	17% of gross income
2 children	25% of gross income
3 children	29% of gross income
4 children	31% of gross income

DON'T FORGET YOUR ADD-ONS

Remember, girlfriends, you are entitled to extra money for other expenses such as day care, babysitting, summer camp and after-school programs. You are also entitled to money for any unreimbursed medical expenses (see Chapter 3). To figure out the exact dollar figure you are entitled to receive from your baby daddy, simply review the amount you have to pay every month for these items then prorate that cost based upon your income and your baby daddy's income. For example, if your baby daddy earns around the same amount of money as you do, then his prorated share of these expenses will be 50% or one half. The other half will be your responsibility. If, however, you are unemployed and have no source of income, then all of the expenses would be left on his shoulders, and you will be responsible for nothing. For an illustration of both methods for calculating child support, see the sample worksheets presented on the next two pages.

SAMPLE CHILD SUPPORT CALCULATION SHEET—
COMBINED PARENTAL INCOME

	MOTHER	FATHER
1.) **MONTHLY GROSS PARENTAL**		
Earnings	_____	_____
2.) **PLUS**		
Rent Received	_____	_____
Dividends from Stocks	_____	_____
Business Profits		

3.) **MINUS**
(If you live in a sate that calculates child support based on gross income only, skip this section and move on to number 5)

	MOTHER	FATHER
FICA	_____	_____
City and State Taxes	_____	_____
Union Dues	_____	_____
Unreimbursed Employee Expenses	_____	_____
Social Security	_____	_____

CONT'D	MOTHER	FATHER
Child Support Paid For Other Children	————	————
Alimony	————	————
4.) EQUALS		
Adjust Gross Income	————	————
5.) ADD BOTH PARTIES' ADJUSTED GROSS INCOME	————	————
6.) MULTIPLY THE COMBINED PARENTAL INCOME BY THE STATUTORY PERCENTAGE BASED UPON THE NUMBER OF CHILDREN INVOLVED	————	————
7.) DETERMINE EACH PARENT'S OBLIGATION BASED UPON THEIR RESPECTIVE EARNINGS	————	————

PLUS

| 8.) ADD ANY ADDITIONAL EXPENSES FOR CHILD CARE AND UNREIMBURSED MEDICAL EXPENSES | ———— | ———— |

SAMPLE CHILD SUPPORT CALCULATION SHEET—
PERCENTAGE OF BABY DADDY'S INCOME

1.) **MONTHLY GROSS PARENTAL**   FATHER'S INCOME ONLY

Income   _____

2.) **PLUS**

Rent Received from Tenant   _____

Dividends from Stocks   _____

Interest from Bank Accounts   _____

Profits from a Business   _____

3.) **MINUS**

FICA   _____

City and State Taxes   _____

Social Security   _____

Child Support Paid
for Other Children,
Alimony   _____

Union Dues   _____

CONT'D   FATHER'S INCOME ONLY

Unreimbursed
Employee Expenses   _____

                    EQUALS

Adjusted Gross Income   _____

4.) MULTIPLY YOUR BABY
DADDY'S INCOME BY THE
STATUTORY PERCENTAGE
BASED UPON THE NUMBER
OF CHILDREN INVOLVED   _____

                    PLUS

5.) ADD ANY ADDITIONAL EXPENSES
FOR CHILD CARE AND UNREIMBURSED
MEDICAL EXPENSES   _____

DEVIATING FROM THE GUIDELINES

Once you find out how much money you are entitled to get based upon your state guidelines, you can decide to accept that amount or demand some higher or lower figure. As long as you and your baby daddy are in agreement, you can be paid just about any dollar amount. The only thing you must do is to state in your written agreement that the two of you have reviewed the guidelines and are aware of your obligations. Following is a sample child support agreement. Use it as the model for the one you write with your baby daddy.

SAMPLE CHILD SUPPORT AGREEMENT

It is hereby stipulated and agreed between the undersigned parties that whereas neither party to this agreement is an infant or an otherwise incapacitated person unable to comprehend the nature of this agreement and the provisions thereof, and whereas neither party has been compelled to sign said document against their own volition,

it is hereby stipulated between the undersigned parties that:

CUSTODY

1. Primary physical custody of the subject child(ren), _____ , shall be with the mother, however, both
(Put your kids' name(s) here) mother and father shall share joint legal custody.

SUPPORT

2. Both parties have read the provisions of the child support standards act of this state and are aware of their obligations pursuant to the same. The parties agree that the father shall pay the mother child support for the subject child(ren) in the amount of _____. Payment to be made according to
(Put amount you agreed to here) the following terms:

    i. Father is to make payment on a _____ basis.
(State weekly, biweekly, etc.)

    ii. Payments are to be forwarded to the mother as follows:

_____

(State whether payments shall be mailed, delivered personally, etc.)

ADDITIONAL EXPENSES

3. The parties agree that in addition to making the above-mentioned payments, the father is to pay for the subject child(ren)'s daycare center fees, dance school fees and summer camp fees. Said payments

are also to be made by means of _____.

(State how payments will be made)

HEALTH INSURANCE

4. The father agrees to maintain the subject child(ren) on his health insurance plan and will pay _____ for all unreimbursed medical expenses not covered by the insurance plan.

LIFE INSURANCE

5. It is hereby agreed between the undersigned parties that the father shall maintain a life insurance policy in the amount of _____. The subject child(ren) shall be named beneficiaries of this policy.

Anywhere, U.S.A (Put your city and state here)

July 25, 2005 (Add current date)

- -

_____   _____

(Mother's Signature)   (Baby Daddy's Signature)

_____

NOTARY PUBLIC

**WHAT TO DO WITH YOUR AGREEMENT
ONCE IT IS COMPLETE**

Once you have finished typing your agreement—remember, handwritten ones are unacceptable—make three copies of the document, have each one signed before a notary public and present them to a clerk at your local family court for filing. Make sure that your agreement is official and will be honored in court if your baby daddy should try to go back on his word in the future, and the only way to do that is by filing it with the court clerk right after the agreement is drawn up. Filing procedures will vary depending upon the state where you live. In some states like New York, to get your agreement filed, you must first petition the court, just as you would in a typical child support case. The court will accept your agreement only after you have been heard before a support magistrate. Other states will be satisfied with you simply filing the document with the clerk's office. Ask the clerk to explain to you in detail the filing procedure for your local court. Listen carefully to what she tells you and follow her instructions to the letter. Failure to do so could hurt you later.

BENEFITS OF A CHILD SUPPORT AGREEMENT

There are a host of benefits that go along with drafting your own child support agreement. Not only can you control the amount of money you get, you can also determine the terms of payment and the number of years your baby daddy will be required to make them. This is because the law permits the parties to decide when the payments should stop. So long as your payment schedule extends to at least your child's eighteenth birthday, a magistrate won't question the legitimacy of your agreement. You can push the age as far as twenty-five or thirty if you choose. All you need is your baby daddy's consent. Another benefit to having your own agreement are all the little tidbits you can get along with your child support. If you seek support through the court, the only additional items you are entitled to receive are funds for add-on expenses, like child care, health insurance coverage and if your man can afford it, life insurance, but with your own agreement you can ask for all of these items plus college tuition, private school fees and even a new car, if your child is old enough to drive. As long as your baby daddy agrees to give these things to you, you can have them. So go for the gusto, girlfriend and make sure you get everything your child(ren) needs.

CHAPTER 8

 CHILD SUPPORT ABUSE

Attorney Middleton,

When I get through with my daughters' father, he will be sorry he ever met me. I want his paycheck garnished, and I want you to serve Mr. Big-time NYPD Detective Man down at the precinct right in front of all of his fellow officers too. Let him feel some of the humiliation I felt when he got married to that prostitute he calls his wife. Would you believe last week, instead of mailing me the $1,200 a month that he usually gives for our girls, he gave it to me in person with that hoochie standing right next to him? The nerve of him. I was good enough to give him two kids but not good enough to marry. Well, I'll fix him. How quickly can you get started on my case?

Lela Douglas

I hate to break the news to you, but it does not appear to me that you have a case. If your children's father is already giving you some $1,200 a month on a police officer's salary, then you are probably already getting more than you are entitled to

receive from him right now. I think that the real reason you want to take this man to court has nothing to do with the needs of your children and everything to do with your desire to punish him for finding someone else. Let go of the feelings you still have for the guy and be thankful that he is a responsible man who did not permit his failure to hold on to you to turn into an excuse to fail as a father.

SEEK CHILD SUPPORT FOR THE RIGHT REASONS

Most women who go after child support do so because they love their kids. They want to provide a better life for them, one where all of their needs are satisfied and at least some of their wishes are met too. Unfortunately, there are a lot of self-centered mamas out there who simply can't be bothered with the needs of their children. For them, child support isn't about blessing their babies, it's about cursing their baby daddy. If their man should spark up a relationship with somebody new, you better watch out. That bitter baby mama is going to come down with child support fever. If he decides to make his relationship permanent, step back because Ms. Thing will soon be bulldozing her way to the family court trying to go after his hard-earned money, and don't let that man have another child. If he does, you can bet your bottom dollar that Sister Child Support Abuser will start screaming her head off about that support check. The poor guy could be a model father who is halfway killing himself to support his children. He might be giving her twice the money she is entitled to plus a little extra for herself, yet none of this will make a bit of difference to the self-centered sister because, after all, it's not the money that she's after, it's an opportunity to bring a good man down.

Recently, my office represented a father of two whose son lived in his house but whose daughter stayed with her mom. As part of an agreement the man had been faithfully paying his ex $180 a week ever since the two split up some seven years ago. Ms. Lady was perfectly fine with this situation—until he moved on with his life and decided to get married. When she heard about his wedding, she went ballistic. Outraged over the fact that he had found love with another woman, she used the strongest weapon she could to fire back at him: a lawsuit for more child support. On the date of the hearing she marched into the courtroom like a runway model, minus the fancy clothes, stomped her foot on the floor and demanded that the $180 payments be doubled to $360. Girlfriend meant business too. She was seeing green and would not be satisfied until all of her ex's money was in her pocket. As the law would have it, however, she ended up walking out with empty hands. It was held by the support magistrate that because the son was living with his father and she was paying no money for him, she was not entitled to the $360 she was demanding for her daughter nor the $180 she had been getting from the man already. That decision stung like the one-two punch of a prize fighter. Not only had she lost her battle for more money, she also had to forfeit the cash that was already coming her way. The trap she had laid for her ex ended up catching her instead.

AVOIDING THE 'TUDE TRAP

Ladies, never allow your emotions to make you look foolish. Stay calm. Keep your cool. Think through your situation and let your brain, not your heart, be your guide. To avoid the 'tude trap that my client's ex fell into, incorporate the following tools into your battle for child support:

1.) If you are angry because your baby daddy has moved on to another woman, don't pretend that it's about the money when it's really about your emotions. Trust me, girl, the first step toward healing from the pain of a past relationship is by embracing personal truth.

2.) Never permit your emotions to block your child's relationship with her daddy. Deal with whatever issues you may have concerning that man through spiritual or clinical counseling.

3.) Be sure to talk with a family-law attorney before you step foot in court over any child support matter. As stated in Chapter 3, a good lawyer will tell you whether you can get the money you are demanding or if you need to abandon your case. If you cannot afford to pay the lawyer's consultation fee, ask her to speak with you for free over the telephone concerning your case. Most lawyers will gladly extend that accommodation to you as long as you limit your conversation to no more than ten minutes and you refrain from rattling on about the unnecessary details of your personal relationship with your baby daddy.

4.) If you cannot find a lawyer who will speak with you for free and you cannot afford to pay a consultation fee for legal advice, take a visit to your state's office of child support enforcement. Although the people there are not attorneys, they often possess a wealth of knowledge on child support issues and may be able to provide assistance to you. To secure the address of the office of child support enforcement in your town, simply contact your telephone directory assistance.

5.) Never discuss your child support issues with your girlfriends. Although they may have good intentions, their homemade advice can cause you more harm than good. Friends have a way of pulling out the drama in a situation and causing your problems to appear worse than they really are.

CHILD SUPPORT IS FOR THE NEEDY, NOT FOR THE GREEDY

Regardless of your financial situation, sisters, keep in mind that the sole purpose of child support is to relieve you of the pressures that accompany raising children, not to help you live like a movie star. I am not saying that every dime you get must be spent directly on the kids, after all the law says you can use child support to cover a host of expenses. Everything from your rent to utilities and even a down payment on a new house can be paid with your child support money, but let's make one thing clear, ladies, it is absolutely wrong for you to throw that money away on overpriced hair weaves, shoes, clothes and other useless junk. I certainly am not trying to offend anyone, but let's face the facts. There are more than a few of us out there who spend those support checks on everything except the children. We will blow it away on our new man, but we won't buy our kids a pair of new shoes. We'll use it for our personal entertainment but never spend a dime for children's books, videos and other items to enhance their education. We'll even buy ourselves the latest designer fashions but will permit our kids to go around town looking like ragamuffins. To all you women who have reduced yourselves to this kind of behavior, I have just one thing to say: you need to check out rapper Kanye West's song "Gold Digger" because it was written just for you.

REDUCING HIM TO A PAY-TO-PLAY DADDY

Another type of abuse that many narrow-minded baby mamas will inflict upon their baby daddys is the denial of access to their children if he fails to pay child support. If for whatever reason a guy is unable to give up the money, this baby mama will yank her kids right out of his life. While such behavior is hurtful to the man who in some cases may have lost his job or is unable to work because of health problems, it is downright devastating to the kids because they can't grasp adult concepts like financial accountability and assume that they are being kept away from their father because they did something wrong. Even worse, if a man has an order of visitation, the failure to give him access to his kids is illegal.

CHAPTER 9

GAMES DEADBEATS PLAY

Attorney Middleton,

My children's father is out of his mind. I think he would rather see me dead than to pay me a lousy $150 a week for our two kids. Last year I had to stop working because I was diagnosed with breast cancer, and despite everything I went through with chemotherapy, surgery and other stuff, he never gave me a dollar or offered to help with the boys. If it weren't for my mother and my three brothers, my kids and I would have landed in a homeless shelter. My cancer is now gone, thank God, but that man is still causing me some major headaches. Believe it or not, he has even threatened to have me arrested for child neglect if I don't stop demanding his money. I know he's trying to get back at me for refusing to take his garbage anymore, but, at this point, I don't care what he does to me. I have been through too much in life to back down now.

Traci Braxton

You go, girl. Don't let his empty threats get to you. As long as you are being good to those children, you have absolutely nothing to worry about. If you beat cancer, I know that you can beat his sorry behind.

THE DEADBEAT GAME

A deadbeat will do just about anything to avoid paying you your child support. No lie is too dirty for him to tell and no act too degrading for him to take. He will shake down his own grandmother if it means he will get away without paying you, so if you really want to get your money out of this guy, you are definitely going to have to gear up for a fight. Brace yourself for the nonstop crap he is bound to shove at you. What's the best way to get ready for his craziness? It's simple: study all the idiotic little games deadbeats love to play. Let's review some of them now.

THE "I'M TAKING THE KIDS" GAME

This is by far the deadbeat's favorite game, so be on the lookout for this one. The object here is for the deadbeat to win legal custody (the right to live with the kids) so that he can put an end to his obligation to pay you child support and force you to pay him. The game usually starts right after he is served with your petition for support. Angered and shocked by your refusal to allow him to ignore his financial responsibility to his children, he will run to court with a bunch of lies about your fitness as a mother and his need to take over the raising of his little ones. He will tell the judge that you are a lousy parent who abuses drugs, alcohol and anything else he can think of. If you have a boyfriend, he will accuse him of molesting your children. He will even blame you for his failure to visit his own kids.

HOW TO SCREW UP HIS GAME

Despite his obvious lies most courts will allow a deadbeat to bring a custody suit and many will even waste needed tax dollars by permitting his case to go to trial, so if you don't want to lose your children you will have to play it smart. Start by being careful about how you handle your kids. No matter how angry you may become, never hit them. Judges frown on corporal punishment and will quickly take your kids away if they fear that they are being physically abused. If you have a boyfriend, never permit him to be alone with your children. This will limit the possibility of your ex accusing him of child molestation. You should also try to keep your kids involved in extracurricular activities. Even if you don't have a lot of money, you can still sign them up for swimming at the YMCA or free classes at your local park or library. If your children are doing poorly in school, hire a tutor for them. You may have to cut back on your hair salon visits in order to pay for the extra help but in the end it will be well worth it. Not only will your children become more well-rounded human beings, but judges favor parents who take an interest in enriching the lives of their little ones.

Another thing that I strongly recommend is that you be very careful about revealing your personal information to your baby daddy. Many women are overly trusting of the men they sleep with and assume that since they are sharing a bed with him, it's also safe to share the intimate details of their lives. Unfortunately most sexual relationships come to an end—sooner or later—and when they do, the last thing you want is for your ex to be walking around with knowledge of your personal business. After all, he could use that information to destroy you and gain custody of your children. I once knew a mother who confided in her baby daddy that she was an illegal alien. Later, when she filed for child support against the man he went straight to immigration officials and tried to have her deported.

THE "I'M NOT THE DADDY" GAME

Denying that he is the father of your children is another popular game among deadbeats. As with all deadbeat games, the object here is to chicken out of paying the support. The difference, however, is that instead of hurting you, he hurts your kids by denying they belong to him. Your child could be practically grown, having known no one else except your baby daddy as her father from the time she was an infant, yet out of nowhere, and despite all the pain it carries, the dead-beat will pop the stupid question: Is this really my child?

HOW TO SCREW UP HIS GAME

As long as you have an order of filiation or a voluntary acknowl-edgment of paternity and your child is at least five years old, winning this game should be pretty easy. Many courts will refuse to entertain a deadbeat's questions concerning his relationship to a child where paternity has already been established and the kid is moving on in years. The deadbeat would need to have some mind-blowing evi-dence against you to get the court to listen to him. If your child is pretty young—under a year old—and the deadbeat should question whether they belong to him, he will be allowed to re-open the pater-nity case so long as he has a good explanation to justify his change of mind. Remember, however, that just because he doubts that he is your child's father doesn't automatically mean that a judge will agree with him. It only means that he will have a right to be heard in court.

THE "YOU CAN'T FIND ME" GAME

This game is usually played by the deadbeat who has more than one home or is able to move around a lot. I also call it the jurisdiction game because the goal is to keep you from serving support papers on him so that the court can get jurisdiction over the case. You see, most deadbeats know that a court can hear a case only after it has obtained authority over the person being sued. That authority is jurisdiction, and the only way to acquire it is by the serving process. If the dead-beat moves around often or has several addresses, serving your papers can get really tricky, making it hard for you to get your money. This is the game that superstar singer Alicia Keys' manager, Jeff Robinson, allegedly played on his ex-girlfriend, Tammy Adams, to avoid paying support for their thirteen-year-old son. Robinson, whose management company MBK Entertainment, reportedly grossed more than $100 million in 2004, is said to have failed to pay child support at all that year. According to Adams, he deliberately delayed court proceedings by first claiming to live in New Jersey then later stating that he had moved to New York. Eventually Robinson was served with papers and today is reportedly making regular support payments.

HOW TO SCREW UP HIS GAME

If your baby daddy is a jurisdiction dodger, don't rely on your personal knowledge about where he may live. Get your local office for child support enforcement to run both state and federal parent locator searches on him. The searches will result in a review of his records from DMV, the Board of Elections, Department of Social Security and his credit report. As long as you properly serve papers upon him at one of the addresses listed on these items, the court will deem your service good and all requirements for jurisdiction satisfied. Parent locator services are available to you whether you have chosen to file your case on your own, through an attorney or with your state administrative agency.

THE "SHE MAKES MORE MONEY THAN ME" GAME

A favorite game of most deadbeats is the "I'm broke, but Mama's laughing all the way to the bank" game. The object here is for him to try to convince a judge that just because you worked your buns off to move up a little in the world while he stayed stuck in one place, he should be exempt from paying support. If your home is bigger than his or your car is nicer than his, get ready, girl. That man is going to whine like a baby that you are a master thief who is stealing all of his money and the court has let you do it because "the system" is always trying to help a woman kick a man while he's down.

HOW TO SCREW UP HIS GAME

The key to winning this game is to bombard the judge with every single bill you have to pay in order to take care of your kids. Every dime you spend for food, clothes, school, camp, babysitting and any-thing else must be made known to the judge. See the list of child-related expenses in Chapter 2. Be sure to bring duplicates of your receipts to court. The magistrate will need a copy for her own files. If you don't have proof of payment for something—for example, your baby sitter is a close friend or family member who you pay by cash, get the person to start drawing up receipts for you as soon as possible. You can also ask her to write a notarized letter stating the services she provides and how much she is paid, but be careful with this. Some magistrates will not accept written statements from a person who is not present in court to be questioned. You may need to ask your baby sitter to actually accompany you to court if you plan to use this option.

THE "I SPEND AS MUCH TIME WITH THE KIDS AS YOU DO" GAME

In this game, instead of being too busy for the kids, the deadbeat wants them all the time. He takes them every weekend and every school vacation. He spends the entire summer with them and would even spend the winter with them if you allowed it. To the outside world he looks like a real dedicated daddy, but trust me, girlfriend, it's not about the kids. It's all about the money. You see, many states grant a reduction in child support when a child spends a large amount of time with the parent who lives away from the child (non-custodial parent). Of course the states vary in terms of the length of time needed in order to qualify for this reduction, but in most instances a visit that is thirty consecutive days long will entitle your baby daddy to a decrease in his child support obligation.

HOW TO SCREW UP HIS GAME

The best way to win this game is by breaking up the time your child spends with her father. Of course your power may be somewhat limited, as the court could impose a visitation schedule on you, however, to the extent possible, keep all long-term visits under thirty days. If he is permitted to have the kids for a month in the summer, try to make the visit three and a half weeks long instead of thirty days. Give him a few extra days for Christmas break in exchange for those lost days during the summer. If he's trying to get the kids for three and a half days out of the week, and you live in a state that recognizes joint custody, cut his time down to two and a half or three days. The idea here is not to keep him away from his kids. It's just to keep him away from your child support checks.

THE "I WILL KIDNAP THE KIDS" GAME

Even though your child may not share a close relationship with her father, unless you have a court order granting you sole custody, the deadbeat can legally snatch her from you at any time. Absent an order for custody, the deadbeat has the same rights to the child that you have, and if he exercises those rights by taking her away from you, he no longer has to pay you that child support.

HOW TO SCREW UP HIS GAME

The obvious way to win this game is by securing an order granting you sole custody of your child as soon as possible. Once you have sole custody, the deadbeat will be arrested and thrown in jail if he attempts to take your child, and he will continue to be obligated to pay you child support.

CHAPTER 10

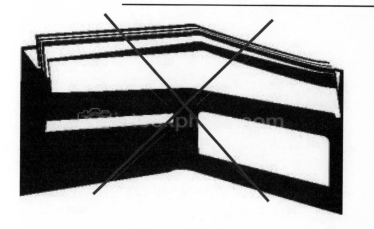

WHEN THE PAYMENTS STOP

Attorney Middleton,

Last week my son's father served me with some ridiculous papers that say he can stop paying me my child support just because the boy enlisted with the Army. I don't know what this is all about, but I'm not about to give up those checks. I need that money to help me pay my mortgage and my son's car note. Plus my son is forever asking me to send him boxes of canned food and snacks because he can't get that stuff on the base. I don't know what his father is going to do, but I refuse to give up my money.

Wanda Hickson

I understand your frustration, and I can see where you might need the additional money, but under the law, when your son enlisted in the Army, he became an adult and, as you know, only children are entitled to child support.

All good things must come to an end, and, unfortunately, child support is no different. Eventually the day will arrive when the checks stop coming in the mail and those extra funds no longer get deposited into your bank account. It is, therefore, crucial, ladies, that you spend support money wisely while it's rolling in and not become so dependent on it that you can't survive when the payments dry up. It is also a good idea to familiarize yourself with the five factors that are sure to result in a "stop payment" on your next child support check. Let's review them.

YOUR CHILD REACHES ADULTHOOD

As a general rule, child support ends on your child's eighteenth birthday. Most states, however, will extend it to age nineteen if the child is still in high school. In New York, child support can extend all the way up to age twenty-one so long as the child is either a student or is unemployed. Of course you and your baby daddy can agree to extend the payments to any age you wish. For more information on child support agreements, review Chapter 7.

YOUR CHILD JOINS THE MILITARY

Once your child enlists in active military service, even if she is under the age of eighteen, you are no longer entitled to child support.

YOUR CHILD BECOMES AN EMANCIPATED MINOR

Your child may be only seventeen years old, but if she leaves your home, cuts all financial ties to you and rebels against your authority, she can be considered an adult under the law.

YOU ALLOW YOUR CHILD TO BE ADOPTED

The adoption of your child by a stepfather frees your baby daddy of his duty to pay you child support. Adoption terminates your baby daddy's responsibilities as a parent and transfers them to the adoptive father. Even if the adoptive father dies, your baby daddy will not be obligated to pay you child support.

YOUR CHILD GETS MARRIED

Once your child gets married, even if she is a minor, she is considered to be an adult under the law, and your baby daddy will no longer be held responsible for supporting her.

YOUR BABY DADDY DIES

In most states, the death of your baby daddy marks the end of his obligation to pay child support. Your child, however, will be entitled to receive her father's Social Security and survivor benefits. If your baby daddy has a life insurance policy naming either her or you as the beneficiary, you will also receive those funds. Additionally, if your baby daddy left a large estate, you may continue to receive monthly payments out of estate assets. But be mindful, girl, those benefits will not be upwardly modified over time like regular child support payments, so whatever amount your child was receiving from her daddy when he was alive, she will continue to receive after he is gone. The mother of Ray Charles' youngest son, Corey, learned this fact the hard way when she reportedly attempted to triple the $3,000 monthly child support award that she had been receiving from the late singer's multimillion-dollar estate. A California court reportedly dismissed her petition and tossed out her case.

YOU KEEP YOUR BABY FROM SEEING HER DADDY

If you intentionally keep your child from seeing her daddy, you may just lose your child support. A court can suspend your payments as punishment for interfering with his right to visitation. Keep in mind, however, that your baby daddy must get the court's approval before he can stop making payments to you.

WRAP-UP

Money doesn't grow on trees and, neither does child support. You have to go after it and hunt it down like an animal in search of prey. At times your quest may be difficult, at other times downright impossible, but if you stay calm and keep your emotions under control, you will be victorious.

To insure that you get all the money you deserve, follow the simple rules laid out in each chapter of this book. Start by finding out whether your man really is your baby daddy (Chapter 1), and with that information in hand move on to determine exactly how much of his money belongs to you (Chapter 2). From there figure out which method you will utilize to get his money (Chapter 3), and if your baby daddy is a deadbeat, do your best to track him down (Chapter 4). Once you find him, make him do right by you (Chapter 5), and if he's a long-distance deadbeat, the same rules apply (Chapter 6). If you have a trustworthy man, consider constructing an out-of-court agreement with him (Chapter 7). Remember no matter how frustrated you may get, never abuse your child support (Chapter 8) and be sure to watch out for the tricky little games that deadbeats play (Chapter 9). Last but not least, be prepared for the day when your child support payments come to an end (Chapter 10). By following these ten simple steps you will reduce stress, save time and experience peace of mind while you get that child support.

GLOSSARY

GLOSSARY

Acknowledgment of paternity: A voluntary consent by your baby daddy that he is your child's father.

Adjudicate: To resolve your case judicially, before a court or administrative officer.

AFDC (Aid to families with dependent children): Public assistance or welfare given to families who are in need of financial assistance because the head of the household is either unemployed, disabled, dead or absent.

Affidavit of service: A written statement made under oath before an authorized officer.

Allegation: An accusation or a claim that has yet to be proved.

Answer: A written response to a summons and complaint that is filed in the court by the defendant in a lawsuit.

Arrears: Past-due child support.

Buccal Swab Test: The procedure in which DNA is matched for the purpose of determining whether a biological relationship exists between two parties. The inner cheek of the parties is gently scraped with a cotton swab to collect cells, which are then compared to see if a match exists between them.

Change in circumstances: A change in the financial condition of either parent that would make a current child support order unfair.

Child support: Money your baby daddy owes you for the support of your child(ren).

(Child Support Enforcement Agency (CSEA): An agency run by the state government that enforces child support orders and assists in the collection of child support awards.

Custodial parent: The person with whom the child lives.

Custody trial: A hearing to determine with whom the child will live.

Deadbeat: A parent who refuses to give financial support to his child(ren).

Default: The failure of a defendant in a lawsuit to answer the allegations contained in a summons and complaint that have been properly served upon him.

Default judgment: A decision made in favor of a plaintiff by a judge or magistrate when a defendant fails to appear in court.

Defendant: A person who has a lawsuit filed against him.

Direct payments: Child support made by your baby daddy to you instead of through child support enforcement.

Downward modification: A court-ordered reduction in the amount of money owed for child support.

Emancipated: The age at which a child becomes an adult and is no longer a parent's legal responsibility.

Federal Parent Locator Service: A government service that uses records from federal agencies to track down a deadbeat dad.

Foreign order: A command for support or paternity issued by a court from another state or country.

Garnishment: A procedure wherein money is taken from your baby daddy as part of a court order to pay past-due child support.

Guideline: A government schedule that establishes how much child support is to be paid by your baby daddy.

Hearing: An appearance before a judge or magistrate by parties in a case for the purpose of resolving their dispute.

Imputed income: Money that is credited to a baby daddy based upon his lifestyle and assets.

Intercept: The taking of a portion of a baby daddy's tax refund, unemployment insurance or disability insurance to pay off past-due child support.

Joint custody: An arrangement where parents share both physical possession and decision-making authority of their child.

Judgment: An order or decision made by a judge or magistrate.

Jurisdiction: The legal authority a court has over a particular person, his property, a geographical area or certain types of cases.

Lien: A legal claim over another person's property that prevents a sale or transfer until a debt is fully satisfied.

Long-arm jurisdiction: The right of a judge or court to claim personal jurisdiction over a person in another state.

Motion: An application to a judge or magistrate to rule on a matter.

Noncustodial parent: The parent with whom the child does not live.

Obligee: The parent who is entitled to receive child support.

Obligor: The parent who is required to pay child support.

Order of filiation: An order that establishes legal fatherhood.

Paternity: Legal fatherhood.

Paternity test: An examination to determine the father of a child.

Petition: A complaint.

Plaintiff: The person who brings a lawsuit against a defendant.

Reciprocity: The procedure by which states and countries agree to cooperate in honoring one another's laws in child support cases.

Retainer fee: Money paid to an attorney for services she provides to a client.

Retroactive child support: Payments that are owed for the time prior to the issuance of an order for support.

Service of process: The delivery of court papers to a person who is part of a lawsuit.

State Parent Locator Service: A government service that utilizes records from state agencies to track down a deadbeat dad.

Subpoena: An official document that orders a person to present certain documents to the court or to make an appearance.

Summons: Written notice to a defendant that he has been sued.

Tax intercept: The taking of a deadbeat dad's tax refund to pay off his child support arrears.

Temporary child support order: Money awarded for a limited time until a permanent award for support can be issued.

Title IV-D agency: Your state office of child support enforcement.

Uniform Interstate Family Support Act (UIFSA): A statute or law that allows you to get child support from a baby daddy who lives in another state or country.

Upward modification: A court-ordered increase in a child support award.

Visitation: The right of a noncustodial parent to spend time with his child.

Wage assignment: A court order that requires your baby daddy's employer to deduct money from his paycheck for child support.

APPENDIX

APPENDIX

STATE CHILD SUPPORT ENFORCEMENT OFFICES

ALABAMA
Alabama Department of Human Resources
Child Support Enforcement Division
P.O. Box 3040000
Montgomery, AL 36130-4000
334-242-9300
Fax-334-242-0606

How child support is calculated: Combines the income of both parents and uses a state schedule of obligations to determine a child support award. Your baby daddy's portion of the obligation is paid to you, but you pay out nothing since the child is in your home.

Modification of child support award: Every three years unless there is an unexpected change in circumstances.

ALASKA

Child Support Services Division

550 W. 7ᵗʰ Avenue, Suite 310

Anchorage, AK 99501-6699

907-269-6900

Fax: 907-269-6650

How child support is calculated: Takes a percentage of your baby daddy's income for child support. To determine an award, the state multiplies his income by the following percentages: 20% (1 child), 27% (2 children), 33% (3 children) and an extra 3% for each additional child.

Modification of child support award: Every three years unless there is a significant change in finances or other unexpected circumstances.

ARIZONA

Division of Child Support Enforcement

Department of Economic Security

P.O. Box 40458

Phoenix, AZ 85067

602-252-4045

Fax: 602-248-3126

How child support is calculated: Combines the adjusted gross income of both parents and uses a state schedule of obligations to determine an exact support award. Your baby daddy's portion of the obligation is paid to you, but you pay out nothing since the child lives in your home.

Modification of child support award: Every three years unless there is a substantial change in financial circumstances.

ARKANSAS

Office of Child Support Enforcement

Central Office Customer Service

P.O. Box 8133

Little Rock, AR 72203

800-262-2445

Fax: 501-682-6002

How child support is calculated: Takes a percentage of your baby daddy's income for child support; uses a preset state schedule to determine an exact support award.

Modification of child support award: Every three years unless there is a substantial change in financial circumstances.

CALIFORNIA

Division of Child Support Services

3701 Power Inn Road

Sacramento, CA 95826

916-875-7400

Fax: 916-875-7499

How child support is calculated: Combines the net income of both parents for child support. To determine an award, the state will multiply the combined parental income by the following percentages: 25% (1 child), 40% (2 children), 50% (3 children). These figures may be adjusted depending upon the amount of time each parent spends with the child.

Modification of child support: Permitted where two years have passed since the last award for support or there has been a substantial change in circumstances.

COLORADO

Division of Child Support Enforcement
1200 Federal Building
Denver, CO 80204
720-944-2960
Fax: 720-944-2660

How child support is calculated: Combines the adjusted gross income of both parents for child support and multiplies that figure with a statutory schedule to determine an actual award. Where the parents share custody, child support is determined by multiplying the adjusted income of each parent with the amount of time they spend with the child.

Modification of child support: Permitted every three years unless there is a substantial change in financial circumstances.

CONNECTICUT

Department of Social Services
Bureau of Child Support Enforcement
25 Sigourney Street
Hartford, CT 06106-5033
800-842-1508
Fax: 860-569-6657

How child support is calculated: Combines the net income of both parents for child support; uses a preset state schedule to calculate an award.

Modification of child support: Permitted every three years unless there is a change in financial circumstances.

DELAWARE

Department of Health and Human Services
Division of Child Support Enforcement
P.O. Box 904
New Castle, DE 19720
302-577-7171
Fax: 302-326-6239

How child support is calculated: Combines the net incomes of both parents for child support; uses a preset state schedule to calculate an award.

Modification of child support: Permitted where at least eighteen months has passed since the last support award.

DISTRICT OF COLUMBIA

Office of Paternity and Child Support Enforcement
Department of Human Services
800 9th Street SW, 2nd Floor
 Washington, D.C. 20024
202-645-5368
Fax: 202-645-4102

How child support is calculated: Takes a percentage of your baby daddy's income and multiplies it with the statutory percentages: 20% (1 child), 26% (2 children), 30% (3 children), 32% (4 or more children). Percentages can increase or decrease depending upon your baby daddy's income level.

Modification of child support: Permitted upon request.

FLORIDA

Department of Revenue

Child Support Enforcement

P.O. Box 8030

Tallahassee, FL 32314-8030

877-769-0251

Fax: 904-414-1698

How child support is calculated: Combines both parents' income for child support; uses a preset state schedule to determine an award.

Modification of a support award: Permitted every three years.

GEORGIA

Department of Human Resources

Office of Child Support Recovery

1718 Peachtree Street

Atlanta, GA 30309-2409

404-206-5362

Fax: 404-206-5460

How child support is calculated: Takes a percentage of your baby daddy's gross income and multiplies it with the statutory percentages. These percentages are: 17%–23% (1 child), 23%–28%, (2 children), 25%–32% (3 children), 29%–35% (4 children), 31%– 37% (5 or more children).

Modification of child support award: Permitted every three years.

HAWAII
Child Support Enforcement Agency
601 Kamokila Blvd., Suite 251
Kapolei, HI 96707
888-317-9081
Fax: 808-587-3717

How child support is calculated: Combines the adjusted gross income of both parents for child support: uses a preset schedule to determine a child support award.

Modification of child support award: Permitted upon request.

IDAHO
Department of Health and Welfare
450 West State Street
Boise, ID 83720-0036
208-334-5500
Fax: 208-334-0666

How child support is calculated: Combines both parents' income and applies that figure to a schedule based upon the number of children in need of child support. If you and your baby daddy share physical custody of your child (he has her at least 35% of the time), the child support payments may be cut in half.

Modification of child support award: Permitted where a modification will change your child support award by at least 15% or fifty dollars.

ILLINOIS

Department of Public Aid
Child Support Enforcement Division
P.O. Box 19404
Springfield, IL 62794
800-447-4278
Fax: 217-524-6049

How child support is calculated: Takes a percentage of your baby daddy's income for child support. Percentages taken are as follows: 20% (1 child), 25% (2 children), 32% (3 children), 40% (4 children), 45% (5 children), 50% (6 or more children).

Modification of child support award: Permitted every three years or where there is an unexpected change in financial circumstances.

INDIANA

Child Support Bureau

Family and Social Services

402 W. Washington Street, Rm. W360

Indianapolis, IN 46204

317-232-3447

Fax: 317-233-4925

How child support is calculated: Combines the gross income of both parents for child support; uses a support table to determine an actual award.

Modification of child support: Permitted where there is an unexpected change in financial circumstances.

IOWA

Department of Human Services

P.O. Box 9218

Des Moines, IA 50306

800-362-2178

Fax: 515-281-6632

How child support is calculated: Takes a percentage of your baby daddy's net income for child support. Uses preset state guidelines to determine an actual award.

Modification of child support award: Permitted where at least two years have passed since prior award for support.

KANSAS
Department of Social and Rehabilitation Services
915 Southwest Harrison Street
Topeka, KS 66612
785-296-3959
Fax: 785-296-2173

How child support is calculated: Combines the income of both parents for child support; uses a preset state guideline to determine a child support award.

Modification of child support: Permitted every two years.

KENTUCKY
Department of Social Insurance
Division of Child Support Enforcement
275 East Main Street
Frankfort, KY 40621
502-564-2285
Fax: 502-564-5988

How child support is calculated: Combines the income of both parents for child support; uses a guidelines worksheet to determine an actual award.

Modification of child support award: Permitted every three years unless there is an unexpected change in financial circumstances.

LOUISIANA

Department of Social Services
District Support Enforcement Office
333 Laurel Street, 2nd Floor
Baton Rouge, LA 70821-0829
800-256-4650
Fax: 225-342-7600

How child support is calculated: Combines the income of both parents for child support; uses a preset state schedule to determine an actual award.

Modification of child support: Permitted every three years unless there is a substantial change in financial circumstances.

MAINE

Department of Human Services
Division of Support Enforcement and Recovery
State House Station 11
Augusta, ME 04333
207-287-3110
Fax: 207-287-2334

How child support is calculated: Combines the gross income of both parents for child support; uses a child support table to determine an actual award.

Modification of child support award: Provides for automatic adjustments to child support awards when the child reaches twelve years of age, eighteen years of age and nineteen years of age. Adjustments can also occur in the award if the child graduates from or is expelled from high school. Other changes are permitted once every three years.

MARYLAND

Child Support Enforcement Administration

311 West Saratoga Street

Baltimore, MD 21201

800-925-4434

Fax: 410-333-8992

How child support is calculated: Combines both parents' actual income for child support; uses a preset state schedule to determine an actual award.

Modification of child support award: Permitted every three years unless there is an extraordinary change in circumstances.

MASSACHUSETTS

Department of Revenue

Child Support Enforcement Division

P.O. Box 4068

Wakefield, MA 01880-3095

617-213-1000

Fax: 617-246-3856

How child support is calculated: Takes a portion of the combined gross income of both parents for child support based upon a sliding scale percentage (plus or minus 2%), depending upon the number of children involved. This state can reduce your child support payments where you and your baby daddy share custody of your child.

Modification of child support: Permitted every three years or sooner where a new award would result in at least a 20% difference in the amount already being received for child support.

MICHIGAN
Office of Child Support Recovery
Family Independence Agency
P.O. Box 30478
Lansing, MI 48909-4980
517-335-0892
Fax: 517-373-4980

How child support is calculated: Combines the net income of both parents for child support; uses a state child support table to determine an actual award.

Modification of child support award: Permitted every two years unless there is an extraordinary change in financial circumstances.

MINNESOTA
Department of Human Services
Child Support Enforcement Division
444 Lafayette Road
St. Paul, MN 55155-3846
888-234-1208
Fax: 612-297-4450

How child support is calculated: Takes a percentage of your baby daddy's net income for child support; uses a preset state schedule to determine an actual child support award.

Modification of child support: Permitted every three years.

MISSISSIPPI
Department of Human Services
Division of Child Support Enforcement
750 North State Street
Jackson, MS 39205
800-345-6347
Fax: 601-359-4415

How child support is calculated: Takes a percentage of your baby daddy's adjusted gross income for child support. Multiplies the income by the following percentages to determine an actual award: 14% (1 child), 20% (2 children), 22% (3 children), 24% (4 children), 26 % (5 or more children).

Modification of child support: Permitted every three years unless there is an extraordinary change in financial circumstances.

MISSOURI
Division of Child Support Enforcement
2701 West Main Street
Jefferson City, MO 65102-1527
573-751-4224
Fax: 314-751-1257

How child support is calculated: Combines the gross income of both parents for child support; uses a preset state schedule to determine an actual award.

Modification of child support: Permitted every three years unless there is an extraordinary change in financial circumstances.

MONTANA

Department of Public Health and Human Services
Child Support Enforcement Division
3975 North Montana, Suite 112
Helena, MT 59620-2943
406-442-7278
Fax: 406-444-1370

How child support is calculated: Combines the actual income of both parents for child support; uses a standard basic multiplier to determine an actual child support award.

Modification of child support: Permitted every three years.

NEBRASKA

Department of Health and Human Services
Child Support Enforcement Office
P.O. Box 94728
Lincoln, NE 68509-4728
412-441-8715
Fax: 412-471-9455

How child support is calculated: Combines the adjusted gross income of both parents for child support; uses a support table to determine an award, based upon the number of children.

Modification of your child support award: Permitted where there is a substantial change in the parties' financial circumstances.

NEVADA

Department of Health and Human Services
Division of Welfare and Supportive Services
1470 East College Parkway
Carson City, NV 89706
775-684-0500
Fax: 775-684-0646

How child support is calculated: Takes a percentage of your baby daddy's gross income for child support; multiplies his income with the following statutory percentages to determine a child support award: 18% (1 child), 25% (2 children), 29% (3 children), 31% (4 children) and 2% additional for each child thereafter.

Modification of your child support award: Permitted every thirty-five months.

NEW HAMPSHIRE

Department of Health and Human Services
Office of Child Support
129 Pleasant Street
Concord, NH 03301
800-852-3345
Fax: 603-271-4771

How child support is calculated: Combines the net incomes of both parents for child support; multiples that income by percentages derived from a state table to determine an actual award.

Modification of your child support award: Permitted every three years or upon request.

NEW JERSEY
Department of Human Services
Child Support Enforcement Services
CN 960
Trenton, NJ 08625
609-292-1087
Fax: 609-984-3630

How child support is calculated: Combines the gross income of both parents for child support; multiplies that income by percentages derived from a state table to determine an actual award.

Modification of your child support award: Permitted every three years or sooner in extreme cases.

NEW MEXICO
Human Services Department
Child Support Enforcement Bureau
P.O. Box 2348
Santa Fe, NM 87504-2348
800-585-7631
Fax: 505-827-7285

How child support is calculated: Combines the actual income of both parents for child support; multiplies that income by percentages derived from a state table to determine an actual award.

Modification of your child support award: Permitted where there has been a substantial change in financial circumstances such that a new award for support would result in at least a 20% change in the amount already being received.

NEW YORK

Office of Child Support Enforcement
102 Washington Avenue, 5th Floor
Albany, NY 12210
888-298-4485
Fax: 518-486-3127

How child support is calculated: Combines the adjusted gross income of both parents for child support; multiplies that income by the following statutory percentages: 17% (1 child), 24% (2 children), 29% (3 children), 31% (4 children), 35% (5 or more children).

Modification of your child support award: Permitted every two years unless there has been a substantial change in financial circumstances.

NORTH CAROLINA
Department of Human Resources
Child Support Enforcement
100 East Six Forks Road
Raleigh, NC 27609-7724
919-571-4114
Fax: 919-881-2280

How child support is calculated: Combines the adjusted gross income of both parents for child support; applies that figure to a state child support table to determine an actual award.

Modification of your child support award: Permitted every three years or sooner where there has been a substantial change in financial circumstances that would result in at least a 15% change in your current award.

NORTH DAKOTA
Department of Human Services
Child Support Enforcement Division
600 East Boulevard Avenue
Dept. 325
Bismarck, ND 58507-7190
800-472-2622
Fax: 701-328-2359

How child support is calculated: Takes a portion of your baby daddy's net income for child support; matches his income with a support schedule for the number of children in need of support.

Modification of your child support award: Permitted every three years or sooner where there is a substantial change in financial circumstances.

OHIO

Department of Human Services
Office of Child Support Enforcement
30 E. Broad Street, 32nd Floor
Columbus, OH 43215-3414
614-752-6561
Fax: 614-752-9760

How child support is calculated: Combines the adjusted gross income of both parents for child support; applies that income to a preset state schedule to determine an actual award.

Modification of your child support award: Permitted every three years or sooner where there has been a substantial change in your financial circumstances resulting in at least a 10% change in the amount of money you currently receive.

OKLAHOMA

Department of Human Services
Child Support Enforcement Office
2409 North Kelly Avenue, Rm. 103
Oklahoma City, OK 73111
800-522-2922
Fax: 405-522-2035

How child support is calculated: Combines the gross income of both parents for child support; applies that figure to a preset state schedule to determine an actual award.

Modifications of your child support award: Permitted every three years or sooner where there is a substantial change in your financial circumstances.

OREGON
Department of Justice
Division of Child Support
1495 Edgewater Street N.W., Suite 170
Salem, OR 97304
503-986-6090
Fax: 503-986-6297

How child support is calculated: Combines the adjusted gross income of both parents for child support; applies that figure to a state guideline percentage schedule to determine an actual award.

Modification of your child support: Permitted every two years or sooner where there has been a substantial change in the financial circumstances of the parties.

PENNSYLVANIA
Bureau of Support Enforcement
P.O. Box 8018
Harrisburg, PA 17105
877-727-7238
Fax: 717-787-4706

How child support is calculated: Combines the adjusted net income of both parents for child support; applies that figure to a state guideline based upon the number of children involved to determine an actual award.

Modification of your child support: Permitted every three years where there is a substantial change in the parties' financial circumstances that would result in a significant change in the child support award.

RHODE ISLAND
Department of Human Services
Child Support Services
77 Dorrance Street
Providence, RI 02903
401-277-2847
Fax: 401-277-6674

How child support is calculated: Combines the income of both parents for child support; applies that figure to state guideline schedule to determine an actual award.

Modification of your child support award: Permitted annually or sooner if a substantial change in financial circumstances has occurred.

SOUTH CAROLINA
Department of Health
Child Support Enforcement Division
P.O. Box 1469
Columbia, SC 29202-1469
800-768-5858
Fax: 803-737-6032

How child support is calculated: Combines the adjusted gross income of both parents for child support; applies that figure to a state guideline schedule based upon the number of children involved to determine an actual award.

Modification of your child support award: Permitted every three years or sooner where there has been either a substantial change in circumstances or the parties have decided to share custody of the child(ren).

SOUTH DAKOTA
Department of Social Services
Division of Child Support
700 Governor's Drive
Pierre, SD 57501
800-286-9145
Fax: 605-773-6834

How child support is calculated: Combines the net income of both parents for child support; applies that figure to a state guideline schedule based upon the number of children involved to determine an actual award.

Modification of your child support award: Permitted where at least thirty-five months have passed since the last order for support was awarded.

TENNESSEE

Offices of Child Support Services
Department of Human Services
Citizens Plaza Bldg., 12th Floor
400 Deaderick Street
Nashville, TN 37248-7400
615-313-4880
Fax: 615-532-2791

How child support is calculated: Takes a percentage of your baby daddy's net income for child support. The state uses the following statutory percentages to determine an actual child support award: 21% (1 child), 32% (2 children), 41% (3 children), 46% (4 children), 50% (5 or more children).

Modification of your child support award: Permitted every three years or sooner where a new award would result in at least a 15% change from the old award.

TEXAS

Office of the Attorney General
Support Services Division
P.O. Box 12017
Austin, TX 78711-2017
800-252-8014
Fax: 512-834-9695

How child support is calculated: Takes a percentage of your baby daddy's net income for child support; applies the following statutory percentages to determine an actual award: 20% (1 child), 25% (2 children), 30% (3 children), 35% (4 children) , 40% (5 children), 40% (6 or more children).

Modification of your child support award: Permitted every three years unless there is an extraordinary change in financial circumstances or where your baby daddy has possession of your child thirty days in a row for any given year.

UTAH

Office of Recovery Services
Bureau of Child Support Services
515 East 100 South
Salt Lake City, UT 84102
800-662-8525
Fax: 802-244-1483

How child support is calculated: Combines the adjusted gross income of both parents for child support. Applies that figure to a state child support table to determine an actual award.

Modification of your child support award: Permitted every three years or sooner if there has been a substantial change in the parties' circumstances.

VERMONT

Agency of Human Services
Office of Child Support
103 South Main Street
Waterbury, VT 05671-1901
800-786-3214
Fax: 802-244-1483

How child support is calculated: Combines the gross income of both parents for child support; applies a state guideline to determine an actual award.

Modification of child support: Permitted where at least thirty-four months have passed since the last order for support was awarded or sooner where there has been an unexpected change in financial circumstances or at least three years have passed since the last child support order was issued by the court.

VIRGINIA

Department of Social Services
Division of Child Support
7 N. Eighth Street
Richmond, VA 23219
804-726-7000
Fax: 804-692-1405

How child support is calculated: Combines the gross income of both parents for child support; applies that figure to a state child support table to determine an actual award.

Modification of your child support award: Permitted where there has been an extraordinary change in financial circumstances.

WASHINGTON STATE
Department of Social and Human Services
Department of Support Enforcement
P.O. Box 45130
Olympia, WA 98504-5130
800-737-0617
Fax: 360-586-3094

How child support is calculated: Combines the net income of both parents for child support; applies that figure to a state child support guideline to determine an actual award.

Modification of your child support award: Permitted where at least three years have passed since the last order was entered by the court and a change in the award would result in at least a 25% increase in the amount of support received.

WEST VIRGINIA
Department of Health and Human Resources
Bureau of Support Enforcement
Resources State Capital Complex
Building 6, Room 817
Charleston, WV 25305
304-558-3608
Fax: 304-558-1121

How child support is calculated: Combines the net income of both parents for child support; applies the figure to a state child support worksheet to determine an actual award.

Modification of your child support: Permitted where there has been a substantial change in financial circumstances.

WISCONSIN
Bureau of Child Support
Division of Economic Support
P.O. Box 7935, Room 382
Madison, WI 53707-7935
608-267-0924
Fax: 608-266-4828

How child support is calculated: Takes a percentage of your baby daddy's income for child support; applies the following statutory percentages to determine an actual award: 17% (1 child), 25% (2 children), 29% (3 children), 31% (4 children), 34% (5 or more children).

Modification of your child support award: Permitted where at least three years have passed since the last order was entered or if an unusual change in financial circumstances has occurred.

WYOMING
Child Support Services
Child Support Enforcement Section
2020 Carey Avenue, Suite 601
Cheyenne, WY 82801
307-635-3365
Fax: 307-777-3693

How child support is calculated: Combines the net income of both parents for child support; applies that figure to a state child support guideline to determine an actual award.

Modification of your child support order: Permitted where there has been a substantial change in financial circumstances, or if at least six months have passed since the order for support was entered and a new award would result in a 20% change in the amount of support being received.

COUNTRIES THAT HAVE AGREEMENTS WITH THE UNITED STATES TO HONOR AMERICAN CHILD SUPPORT ORDERS

Australia

Bermuda

Canada

England

France

Jamaica

Norway

South Africa

United Kingdom

INDEX

INDEX

A.

Acknowledgment of paternity, 24

Add-on expenses, 30

Adoption and child support, 137

Adulthood and child support, 136

Affidavit of service, 20

Alumnae association, 76

B.

Bankruptcy, 49

Benefits of a child support agreement, 113

Benefits of establishing paternity, 25

Birth certificate, 25

Buccal swab test, 22

C.

Child-related expenses, 31

Child's standard of living, 34

Child support agreement, 102-110

Child support arrears, 63

Child support defined, 30

Child support magistrate, 21, 62

Complexity of your case, 59

Court day, 59

Court process, 21

Credit report, 76

Criminal records, 75

D.

Daddy's potential income, 49

Daddys who report no income, 44–47

Deadbeats who flee the country, 94

Deadbeat game, 126–132

Death and child support, 137

Declaration of paternity, 25

Department of Motor Vehicles, 73

Defining income, 44

Discount parternity testing, 23

DNA, 22

Documents agency needs to file for child support, 54

E.

Emancipated minor, 136

F.

Former employer, 73

Friends and family (your baby daddy's), 73

G.

Garnishment of wages, 82

Garnishment of property, 83

Genetic marker test, 22

Government locator service, 75

H.

Handling your child support case on y our own, 51

Hidden assets, 84

Hiring an attorney, 56

How your baby daddy earns his money, 58

Houses and other property, 84

I.

Income shares formula, 36–37
Inheritance, 26
Insurance coverage, 26

J.

Jail time, 85
Jobless daddy, 48

K.

L.

License, 74
License suspension, 85
Long-arm jurisdiction, 93

M.

Marriage and child support, 137
Marriage and paternity tests, 21
Marshal, 20
Military enlistment and child support, 136
Modifying a child support award, 63–64
Mommy and daddy's income, 33
Monthly household expense sheet, 32
Most-wanted deadbeats, 86

N.

Neighbors, 74
New woman's income, 48

O.

Order of filiation, 22, 25

P.

Paternity, 19, 60

Paternity acknowledgement forms, 24

Paternity test, 22–23

Paycheck, 81

Percentage of income formula, 39

Petition, 19

Previous court orders, 61

Process server, 20

Property garnishment, 81

Proof of child-related expenses, 61

Q.

R.

Retroactive child support, 63

S.

Sample child support agreement, 111

Sixteen things every baby mama must know about her baby daddy, 70–71

State guidelines, 35

State agency method of filing for child support, 54

Summons, 19

T.

Taxes, 50

Tax interception, 82

Temporary child support, 62

U.

Uniform Interstate Family Alert Support Act (UIFSA), 90–92
United States Department of Agriculture, 30

V.

Vasectomy, 87
Voluntary acknowledgment of paternity, 24
Voluntary declaration of paternity, 25

W.

Wage withholding, 81

X.

Y.

Your baby daddy's other kids, 35

Z.

FOOTNOTES

Chapter 2.

1. Simone Spence, *Deadbeats: What Responsible Parents Need to Know About Collecting Child Support* (Naperville, Illinois: Sourcebooks Inc., 2000)

2. Ibid, p. 85.

Chapter 3

3. Ibid, p. 85.

Chapter 4

4. Ibid, p. 81.

5. Ibid, p. 81.

6. Ibid, p. 81.

7. Ibid, p. 88.

8. Ibid, p. 88.

9. Ibid, p. 88.

10. Ibid, p. 84.

11. Ibid, p. 85.

12. Ibid, p. 105.

Chapter 5

13. Ibid, p. 106.

14. Ibid, p. 106.

15. Ibid, p. 107.

16. Ibid, p. 107.

17. Ibid, p. 109.

18. Bonnie M. White and L. Douglass Pipes: *Child Support Survival Guide: How to Get Results Through Child Support Enforcement Agencies* (Franklin Lakes, N.J., Career Press, 1997).

DISCLAIMER

The material contained in this book is for information purposes only. It is not intended to serve as legal advice for you or to replace the advice of an attorney. Before following any of the recommendations in this book, please consult a lawyer licensed to practice in the state where your case will be heard.

Please also be aware that the laws that govern child support are constantly changing, therefore, all statutes that have been quoted in this book may no longer be good law by the time you read this book.

ABOUT THE AUTHOR

Cathy Middleton is a family law attorney with a specialty in child support matters. She has successfully handled hundreds of child support cases and won over a million dollars in child support awards. Middleton has traveled extensively giving legal advice to single parents. She also conducts child support seminars at colleges and universities.

Middleton has appeared as a guest on the nationally syndicated *Wendy Williams* radio show and *The Andy Anderson Live Show.* She has also been quoted in *Essence Magazine* and has been featured in *Ebony Magazine's 50 Leaders of the Future.*

Middleton holds a Juris Doctorate degree and an LL.M degree from Temple University School of Law. She also attended Howard University. Middleton lives in New York with her husband, attorney Gregory Lewis, and her daughter, Shelby.

To contact Cathy Middleton, e-mail her at Middlewis@aol.com